JESUS IN THE FAITH OF CHRISTIANS

By the same author

THE ELUSIVE MIND
OUR EXPERIENCE OF GOD
FREEDOM AND HISTORY
THE SELF AND IMMORTALITY
PERSONS AND LIFE AFTER DEATH
THE PHILOSOPHY OF RELIGION
MORALS AND REVELATION
MORALS AND THE NEW THEOLOGY
CONTEMPORARY BRITISH PHILOSOPHY, Vols 3 and
    4 (ed.)
PHILOSOPHY EAST AND WEST (ed.)
CLARITY IS NOT ENOUGH (ed.)

JESUS IN THE FAITH OF CHRISTIANS

Hywel D. Lewis

First published 1981 by
THE MACMILLAN PRESS LTD
London and Basingstoke
Companies and representatives
throughout the world

ISBN 0–333–29105–0

Photoset in Great Britain by
ROWLAND PHOTOTYPESETTING LTD
Bury St Edmunds, Suffolk
and printed in
Hong Kong

Contents

Preface

This book contains the Laidlaw Lectures delivered at
Knox College, Toronto, in the autumn of 1979. Its main
concern is to stem the more extreme forms of the tendency
to demythologise the central themes of the Christian
Religion, and I have adopted the method, best suited it
seemed to me for public lectures, of singling out a few of
the more prominent and skilled of the proponents of that
view, for relatively detailed discussion, rather than
attempt a more comprehensive survey. There are aspects
of the subject which I have not been able to treat in the
limit I set myself, but I thought it more advantageous on
the whole to publish this brief statement of the difficulties
a Christian encounters in some of the very influential
recent statements of central Christian themes than to
enlarge the present lectures in a form which would be
bound to overlap with the third of the volumes based on
my Gifford Lectures which I have in preparation to
succeed the sequel to *The Elusive Mind* and which I hope
will be available through the kindness of the same
publisher very soon.

I am much indebted to my friend, Professor H. P.
Owen, for reading through the lectures before they were
delivered, and to Miss Betty Wood, at King's College,
London, for her help in preparing the final draft for the
printers and correcting the proofs.

Lecture 1 draws extensively on my own summary of my
views on religious truth which was given as a Presidential
address to a conference of the International Society for
Metaphysics meeting at Jerusalem in August 1977. By
kind permission of the officers of the Society I have kept

close to the form in which the lecture was originally delivered to them. Appendix A to Lecture 3 is reproduced from an extract to an earlier address given at Oxford and published in *The Modern Free Churchman* for the Spring of 1973. I am grateful for permission to do this and also to include, as Appendix B to Lecture 3, one of the series of Saturday morning articles I wrote for *The Times* in the summer of 1969. I have also drawn in Lecture 4 on material given in an address to the General Assembly of the Presbyterian Church of Wales and printed in *Y Traethodydd*.

My final and very pleasant duty is to thank Principal J. C. Hay and his colleagues for the honour they did me in asking me to give these lectures and for the quite outstanding hospitality and kindness of all concerned which was extended to my wife and myself during our stay in Toronto and in the course of shorter visits for lectures for the philosophers and the theologians at places made dear to me by earlier teaching assignments, namely Boston University and Yale. There can be no way in which one can adequately acknowledge such good will. If the publication of the lectures goes some way towards achieving this I shall certainly be delighted.

Hywel D. Lewis

1 Religious Experience and Truth

The notion of religious experience appears to me central to all discussions of major religious issues today. It is, however, a notion about which there appears to be a great deal of confusion and misunderstanding. There are terms like 'Nature', or 'Freedom', which admit of such a wide variety of interpretation (some of them sharply contradictory) that their use tends to become almost pointless. 'Religious experience' is apt to fall into this class. It is sometimes used to refer to any religious activity or practice whatsoever, and thus to become quite otiose. This is the use that some have in mind when they say that they have never had a religious experience: they just mean that they are agnostics. For others 'religious experience' means some very peculiar type of experience, like having visions or hearing voices, or having a distinctively mystical experience. For some the term is associated, with some but only very limited justification, with an excessively emotional religious indulgence. In its main use, and in the profound importance ascribed to it by devout persons in all ages, the term stands for none of these things. It is important therefore to indicate just what we should normally understand by 'religious experience'. I shall attempt to do this as fairly as I can within a limited space, and I shall also try to give a brief indication of how this relates to other major concerns.

I shall waste no time over those who think of religious experience primarily, and perhaps exclusively, in terms of paranormal phenomena. Such occurrences need not in fact be properly religious at all. To what extent they may be I have discussed at some length in Chapters xiv and xv

of my *Our Experience of God*.[1] Those who have had paranormal experiences in the context of their religious life,
ascribe importance to them only in relation to other
aspects of their faith; usually they minimise their importance and treat them as quite peripheral to their
essential commitment. This is why it seemed to me so
unreasonable for a critic of the standing of Alasdair
MacIntyre, in a well-known book[2] some years ago, to make
such heavy weather over claims to have had visions of the
Virgin Mary etc. Did she 'speak Aramaic', did she 'remember Galilee'? Questions of this kind seem to me to
show a total, indeed obtuse, insensitivity to what religion
is essentially like, even in the contexts where visions and
voices and other forms of 'the marvellous' are in fact
invoked.

But we must be especially careful not to think of
religious experience merely in terms of some features of
human experience as a whole, or some generalisations or
deductions from what our situation as human beings is
like. Religious experience, in essentials, is not incipient
metaphysics, however important it may be for metaphysical reflection. Its peculiar significance derives from
its being a distinctive experience which people undergo,
as they may have a moral or an aesthetic experience. This
does not mean that it is always easy to recognise or
delimit, as in the case, for example, of some forms of pain.
But it would be quite wrong to identify it with features of
experience which all can recognise, or with neutral
occurrences to which some further religious significance
may be ascribed. Religious experience is essentially
religious; a distinct ingredient, to my mind a vital one, in
an essentially religious awareness, and identifiable as
such.

I go out of my way to stress this because of a prevailing
tendency, in current philosophy of religion, to think that
so much of religion is initially neutral, even the sense of
the numinous, according to some. In my view, we cannot
produce any proper form of religion out of non-religious
elements. There is indeed a place for the interpretation of
experience; perception, for example, looks very different

as the philosopher considers some of its extraordinary features. The last thing I wish to do is to discourage reflection on religious awareness, or to present it as a raw datum which some may accept, others not, and no more. We need in fact to think more carefully about it than anything else in religious commitment at present. But we must not, in the process, so dilute it that it is nothing recognisable in and for itself.

The same goes for some fashionable views which equate religious experience with an alleged contentless relation with God sometimes known as an 'I-Thou relation'. I have a very great regard for Martin Buber, and I wish more heed were paid by those who refer to him to my fairly close discussion, in Chapter XII of *The Elusive Mind*,[3] of what emerges in a positive way from all that he had to say on this theme. But I make no sense whatsoever, in human or in divine relationships, of a mere relation to which no kind of distinctive precise significance can be attached. The nearest we get to this is the insight or intuition into the inevitability of there being God, and of this I shall say more shortly. But an encounter which is no particular kind of encounter, a 'meeting' which cannot be characterised in any way, appears to me to be just nothing. To make the invocation of it a way of by-passing all the hard epistemological problems is just an escape from our intellectual responsibility; it plays into the hands of contemptuous agnostics.

For related reasons I dismiss all accounts of religious experience in exclusively emotional terms. Emotion plays its part, but the core of religious experience, I submit, is essentially cognitive. How then should we understand it?

At the centre, it seems to me, is the enlivened sense of the being of God—or, if that at this stage is too theistic a term, of some supreme transcendent reality—as involved in the being of anything at all. This is what lies behind the traditional arguments. We all know their inadequacy as arguments, notwithstanding all the refinements attempted in recent times. But they still haunt us, and this seems to me to be because they reflect in different ways the conviction that there can be no ultimate fortuitousness in the being of things. We seek explanations of the way things are, not as a mere psychological compulsion but as rational beings. We do not give up when no sort of explanation is possible—we insist that it must be available somewhere; but no finite explanation is fully adequate, each proceeds in terms of the way we actually find that things cohere, and there remains the question why they should be this way at all, or why anything at all should exist. We can, at least without sheer inconsistency, say that it all just happened, that somehow things began to *be* out of a total void and took the remarkable course which enables us to manipulate and understand our environment, in terms of perfect concomitant variation even to the astonishing vastness and complexities of macroscopic and microscopic science of today. We may not contradict ourselves if we say that all this just came into being out of nothing, but is it credible? Why should anything start up at all, much less take the remarkable intelligible shape things have, out of just nothing? On the other hand it is equally unintelligible to suppose that the world has always been, that in no sense has there been any sort of origination. 'Always' in this sense becomes meaningless. Aeons beyond all computation, and certainly beyond imaginative realisation, we can at least comprehend, but a strictly infinite past is just not intelligible.

It is these radical antinomies that compel us to recognise some more ultimate reality in which all that we can, in principle, comprehend is rooted, but which is not itself comprehensible beyond the recognition of its inevitability; a mystery, not partial but total, in which everything there is is invested, but not the mystery of more bewilderment, the mystery of real transcendent being.

Philosophers put this in fairly sophisticated terms. But the sense of it, however imperfectly expressed, does not require great sophistication. It is elicited in various ways, not least by what Jaspers has called 'limit situations', and I myself have ventured elsewhere to indicate in more detail how the sense of the transcendent awakens in the minds of the most naive as well as of sophisticated persons and societies. It can be traced back as far as recorded history goes. Art and practice as well as intellectual reflection involve it. But granted some intimation in this way of a supreme or transcendent reality, how do we go from there?

It is at *this* point that I would wish to invoke the idea of religious experience. I wish to stress very much that I do not appeal to the notion of religious experience as such to establish the existence of God, least of all in the naive form of insisting that there must be God because we experience him. That would clearly not do without indication of the sort of experience this is and how it is warranted. It would be a gigantic begging of the question. Religious experience properly comes in at the point where we ask how we go further than the sense of some ultimate all-encompassing mystery involved in all that we are or find.

There are of course some who do not seek to go further. They stay at the sense of profound wonderment at the essentially incomprehensible source of all there is, sometimes almost to the point of the repudiation of finite being. In actual practice religion has rarely been able to remain at this rarefied level. Present existence claims its rights and our attention. Finite existence cannot be denied any more than the infinite, even if it finds no better place than some mode or articulation of the infinite. At some level there appear, from the remotest times to our own, particular practices, attitudes, obligations, varied and suggestive symbolism, all intimating that the sacred which, in one sense, we cannot approach and whose essential mystery we cannot fathom, is nonetheless peculiarly present, 'in thy mouth and in thy heart', as one scripture puts it, that it involves a way of life for us, a purpose, a formative influence in personal and social history, a meaning and a presence articulating itself in all manner of ways and leading, in some instances, to highly refined formulations of belief, even to the curiously presumptuous intimacy of petitionary prayer. Men speak of meeting God, of 'walking' with him, of hearing his voice, of turning away from him, of encountering his wrath and, in the same awareness almost, finding him a seeking, reconciling God who draws all men to their ultimate fulfilment 'in him'. They even speak of God incarnate as a living, limited finite creature who died in a scandalously shameful way. How is any of this to be warranted, affirmed or rejected? What meaning can it have?

It is here, in my view, that religious experience is the seminal and vital consideration. I do not, of course, wish to deny that the 'insight' into there having to be God, along the lines indicated, is itself an experience. But it is so in the sense that all cognition is experience. To apprehend that twice two is four, or that the angles of a triangle add up to 180 degrees, is experience. But no one would claim, in these cases, that we know from ex-perience, on the basis of what we find or observe, that these things are so, as we know that grass is green and fire is hot. 'The appeal to religious experience', as it is sometimes called, is not a strictly empirical one, in the sense of empiricism which confines it to presentations of sense, but it has more in common with it than strictly *a priori* knowledge. Certain things are claimed on the basis of certain things that have happened.

The one qualification of this, and it is a vital one, is the point already noted, namely that, at the core of religious experience, is the enlivened insight into the being of God. We do not know this because things happen in any particular way, but, essentially, because they happen at all. The insight involved is peculiar but certainly not quasi-empirical. On the other hand, the enlivening of this insight in peculiar conditions, and the repercussions of it on other crucial aspects of particular experiences, seem to me to be the raw material out of which all other genuine religious awareness is built—and by which it is tested.

At this point there is a very close analogy between the way we know one another and the way we know God. We do not know the existence of other persons generally in any *a priori* or in any intuitive way, though some phil-osophers make that strange claim. We know all we know about other persons, I submit, in some mediated way, however close and intimate this may be. Without some evidence we would not know the existence of anyone. But the being of God we know quite differently, as indicated. It is in no sense a matter of evidence as this usually goes. But *all the rest is*, and it is along these lines that I, at least, react to the familiar challenge of empiricist critics—what would count for or against your belief? For the existence of God, I answer 'Nothing'. It is not that kind of aware-ness: it is a quite peculiar insight about which nonetheless much may be said, again along the lines indicated. But for all other affirmations, the live particularisation of pro-found devotion, we turn to specific evidence, to what counts for or against, to what can, in some respects at least, be analysed and set forth, though by no means in exclusively sensible terms.

I make a special point of stressing this, as so many who are concerned about religion, at highpowered profes-sional levels or more simply, fall back before the fashion-able challenge on either blind appeals to authority or some vague noncognitive attitude or commitment for which there is no rational justification. Interest in religion may be revived today, in fleeting and transitory ways, by simple-minded appeals to emotion or hysteria or palli-atives to those who hunger for spiritual sustenance—or we may make do for a while with attenuations which but thinly disguise the essential secularity of our attitudes. But this will not last. Religion needs justification, most of all in a sophisticated age like our own. No great religion can survive without it.

It is this justification of what is distinctive in the claims of the great religions, and the means of assessment and the basis of dialogue, that is to be found essentially, in my view, in religious experience, rightly understood. The points of convergence as well as the differences can be much better understood in these terms and a means made possible of maintaining our distinctive stances while entering with genuine empathy and appreciation into the religious devotion of others. It will also be a very great gain indeed, in all religions, to show that we are fully equipped to confront the demand for justification and fully take the point of empiricist critics, though by no means entirely on their own terms.

Let us return, then, to the question of what a religious experience involves besides the enlivened sense of the being and mystery of God. I want first to add here that, if the transcendent is to function adequately as the ultimate answer to our 'why questions', or as explanation in the very special elusive sense indicated, it must be deemed to be complete and adequate in all respects in itself; in other words perfect, in the evaluational sense as well as self-sustaining. I do not see how anything less than supreme perfection could meet the case, and in this context I would like to refer you to a quite admirable, but not I suspect sufficiently regarded, book by Professor Sontag entitled *Divine Perfection*.[4] The sense of the holy is essentially evaluational, and does not become so, as is implied in some readings of Otto, by further schematisation. But I must leave this point as it is for our purposes.

The main point to be stressed now is that the sense of ultimate being, mysterious beyond any fathoming in what it must be in itself other than ultimate perfection, has a distinctive impact on other formative features of the total experience in which it occurs. It corrects the perspective in which we view the world around us, it highlights what is of greatest import for us, it makes us see the familiar anew, as in art and poetry; and it does this under the insistent sense of transcendent being unavoidably having its place in our thought. The transcendent claims what it stimulates for its own, and God, whom no man hath seen, the impenetrably holy, removed and remote as infinite being from finite, becomes a closely intimate articulate presence in the very core of our own essentially finite awareness.

The substance of what we come to learn about God in this way is finite. It may present difficulties but no difficulties beyond our understanding and resolving in the normal exercise of finite intelligence. *What* we learn is finite and has no irresolvable mystery in it. Much of it is indeed very simple, however astonishing on occasion. The peculiarly divine factor comes in when these ex-

ceptional insights into our own situation and its require-
ments are seen to be induced in a very sharp way,
deepened and refined, under the impact of the movingly
enlivened sense of the holy and the transcendent. As I
have put it elsewhere, God puts his own imprimatur on
certain insights and sensitivities. He underlines, as it
were, certain things in our experience and writes his own
mind into them. They come to carry his authority
additionally to their own. They are what he specifically
wants us to note. The devout acquire the art of listening
and heeding what is communicated thus within our own
sensitivity and concentration.

One feature of exceptional importance in the process
whereby our understanding is extended in the enlivened
sense of the involvement of our lives in a supreme and
transcendent reality is the refinement and deepening of
moral awareness. It is of great importance that this should
be understood aright. The view has often been advanced
that we cannot ascribe genuine objectivity to ethical
principles unless they are considered to be expressly
dependent on some religious reality. This seems to me to
be dangerous doctrine. It is plain that persons with no
religious awareness or commitment can have profound
appreciation of moral ideals and splendid devotion to
them. There is no inconsistency or logical impropriety in
their being so. The objectivity of morals is autonomous, as
I have stressed myself on many occasions, and some of
the most notable and persuasive defenders of moral
objectivity have been prominent agnostic philosophers
such as G. E. Moore and C. D. Broad. Their case, a very
convincing one to me, does not rest at all on religion.
Ethics has no more direct dependence on religion than
mathematics or science. But this does not preclude
morality from being, as most persons would take it to be,
at the very heart of religion.

It is so not just because the ultimate is also supreme
perfection, and commitment to it is also therefore commitment to what is surpassingly good, but also because it
is in the refinement of ethical understanding, in the
sharpening of conscience as it may more popularly be put,

that the peculiar disclosure of divine intention for us takes place. It is in the voice of our own conscience that the voice of God is most distinctly and significantly heard. This does not make conscience an essentially religious faculty, but it does make it the pre-eminent medium within which the articulation of the mind of God to us takes place. It is here above all that we find our exceptional clue to what God is like and what is our own involvement with and special relation to him.

None of this means that devout people are morally infallible or have a monopoly of all good sense and advance in ethical understanding. There are perversions of religion and profound misunderstandings of its nature that have been very gravely detrimental to ethical good sense and which have from time to time brought religion itself into serious discredit. The refinement of moral understanding involves, moreover, a great deal besides the sharpening of ethical insight as such; it requires sound appreciation of the facts and circumstances in various situations and the over-all consequences of various policies. On these matters the devout may not always be the best authorities and religion certainly confers no immunity from error on matters of fact. Nor does it always carry with it the guarantee of the finest ethical insight as such. The agnostic may sometimes excel in both regards.

What we can say however is that, other things being equal, the enlivened sense of the transcendent carries with it essentially a refinement of moral sensitivity and that it is moreover to this source that the most impressive advances in ethical principles over the years have been due. This is not the place to justify the latter submission in detail. My concern at the moment is more with the general contention that, while it is inherently impossible for us to rise beyond our finite nature and comprehend the being and mind of God as it is for him, we find the incursion of the divine into specific human experience, and thereby a pre-eminent clue into what our relation to it should be, in the peculiarly religious toning and refining of moral experience.

This is not the only example, far from it. We may speak

in similar terms of our appreciation of the world around us and its significance, and of the impetus this has given, among other things, to the advance of science. The artistic attitude is in the same way close to religion here, and each has immensely fructified the other for that reason. But it is not primarily so much a matter of general affinity as of moments of profound religious awareness in which the deepening of religious insight as such takes its course in the blending of itself with perceptions and sensitivity in other secular regards, which thereby afford distinctive matter, apprehensible in the normal secular way by us, out of which the fullness and the richness and the intimacy of genuine religious existence is shaped, and by which it is also corrected and criticised.

Correction and criticism are indeed of very great importance here, for the distinctively religious factor, in a total religious experience, operates upon and within the other secular features of our situation. These often have faults of their own, and this is how it comes about that we sometimes sincerely ascribe to the voice of God items which are only too grievously marked by our own limitations and failings. It would be fine in some ways if the mind of God were disclosed to us in some indelible and wholly unmistakable way, written in the sky or on tablets of stone or of gold in some inscription which is indisputably divine. Dispute, and presumably doubt, would be at an end. But it does not happen that way. Short of being God ourselves, what sanction could we invoke, what are the credentials of a message so conveyed? There is indeed no such way for the voice of God to be heard by finite beings. He speaks in the ways we can understand in his peculiar obtrusion into the normal exercise of the faculties with which he has endowed us. But it is not the mere exercise of finite powers that is involved. There is the peculiar transformation of them which we have the reasons indicated for ascribing to divine intervention in the enlivened sense of the transcendent already described.

A genuine prophet can, for these reasons, be sincerely mistaken, and devout persons have always to be searching out their own minds and hearts to be as sure as they can that what they take to be the voice of God is not the voice of their own errors and failings, or at least tinged by these. That does not preclude firmness of conviction and deliverance. The prophet may speak with authority, but he must be mindful also that he is but a medium, a vessel that is often cracked and broken.

One particular feature of the fallibility of genuine prophetic awareness is the involvement of all of us in the particular circumstances of our age and society. When, as in societies at a relatively low level of moral development, the sense of the divine impinges upon their attitudes, the progress they make will be correspondingly limited and sometimes distorted. If the ethical understanding of a community has not advanced beyond the level of crude retribution and collective guilt, there may well be a genuinely religious ingredient in the perpetuation of ideas which a more enlightened age would find morally abhorrent. What we have to be constantly heeding is the intertwining of genuine religious disclosure and insight with other all too fallible aptitudes and interests of finite creatures. Much in the sacred scriptures of various religions will become more intelligible to us and can be viewed judiciously in their proper setting if we think, as indicated, of divine disclosure as a leaven in the totality of our own aptitudes and aspirations. At the same time the distinctiveness of the transcendent influence must not be lost or wholly merged in the finite media on which it operates.

The precise moment of genuine religious awareness, operating within the functions it claims for its own operation, may not always be easily delimited. It may be sharp, as in sudden conversion; but even in these cases there is often a period of subtle maturing in which truly religious elements come to their open and more explicit formulation. More commonly, although religious aware-ness and sensitivity may be clear and explicit, it has its own ebb and flow, it merges itself in other concentrations of attention, it may be gentle and unobtrusive, in acts of worship or meditation, much as aesthetic awareness is not always easily delimited and isolated from the observations and attentiveness which it takes up into itself. It is for these reasons that some may even fail to detect the moment of live religious awareness or allow it in retrospection to be lost in the media which it embraces. This in particular is where very careful thought is needed in our times to detect and uphold the element of genuine religious awareness against crude and bogus travesties of it.

This is all the more the case because the live religious awareness lives on in other experiences and practices and also perpetuates itself dispositionally in our way of living as a whole. Its occurrence may be known obliquely and indirectly, and this in notable cases is no mean assurance of its presence. It may well become apparent by its fruits. But we can never rely on that alone. The enlivened individual awareness is the indispensable religious factor, and it is out of it pre-eminently that the distinctively religious shape of any faith is formed.

In my fuller discussion of these matters, in my book *Our Experience of God*, I also ascribed particular importance to what I described as the patterning of religious experience. There are significant recurrences and variations which I sought to describe. It has often been found, for example, that the enlivened awareness of transcendent being often comes about in situations where we have the least justification for expecting it, for example in states of an overwhelming sense of guilt. The latter, especially a sense of grievous wrong-doing, comes between us and one another and between us and God; it drives us on our own inner resources which dry up without the sustaining sense of the world around us and of other persons. It is in this debility that we find the real penalty of sin. But, surprisingly, it is often in just this situation of despair and desperation that men have found the onset of the renewed awareness, sometimes gentle, sometimes disturbing, of infinite being as the end and sustainer of their own existence, and life as a whole becomes renewed again and transformed. The recurrence of this, its variations and the extension of it into the religious consciousness of various

societies, builds itself up over the ages into the sense of
God, not as mere remote sustainer or 'Unmoved Mover',
but as a seeking, reconciling God peculiarly involved in
what we are and in our relationship with him. This is, to
my mind, a very important aspect of the emergence of the
more theistic forms of religion.

The same may be said of other situations of desperation,
whether we bring them on ourselves or not. It does not
follow that distressing circumstances and evil are straight-
way resolved. Appalling evil is still with us and presents
the severest tension and strain for religious commitment.
It is a problem I cannot lightly deviate into now. But in
these situations also people have found the sustaining
and recurring sense of God invading their attitudes as a
whole and giving them renewal of strength. God comes to
be known as 'an ever present help in trouble'.

My submission, without pursuing any of these illustra-
tions in further detail here, is that it is in the substance
and the patterning, which I would also much stress, of the
moulding and refining of otherwise neutral sensitivities
and attitudes by the insistent impact of the transcendent,
rather than in *a priori* and essentially empty attempts to
determine abstract properties of God, that we find the
vindication and shaping, as well as the appropriate
critique, of the more particular affirmations and practices
of actual living religions. The parallel with 'other minds' is
here very close. We do not, as I have persistently maintained elsewhere, know the minds of other persons as we
know our own; however close our relationships may be,
however intimate, there is an essential element of mediation. The relation we have with God is no less intimate
and close because it comes in the mediation of the peculiar
modification of our own experience: it is as close as finite-
infinite relationships can be, and to those who experience
it profoundly there is no barrier that matters.

For many who persist in an agnostic or sceptical view of
religion I suspect that a major determinant of their
attitude is the expectation that religion must vindicate
itself for them, if at all, in some form of supernatural
experience of which finite beings are not capable at all.

This is the sophisticated version of the expectation that the astronauts may discover God for us. What we need is to know better where and how to look, and to persevere more in the demanding discipline of looking in the right way. Far too often we take it all to be a matter of a few formal considerations one way or the other when in fact it is a matter of living committed lives in the closest association with the witness of profound experience over the ages.

Closely related to the same mistake is the supposition that religious experience is essentially and wholly a private matter. It has to be initially and in itself private, but what matters most is not the intimations of God that we may chance to have in our more exclusively private existence, but rather the absorption into our individual awareness of the wealth and significance of the sustained and developing religious awareness of men down the ages. It is not in a void that we encounter God but in all the rich diversities of our cultures and the formative part of religion within them. This is what must come alive for us in our individual experience.

This is what is sustained for us in various ritual and symbolic practices. How these function, and where they are genuine and healthy, is a subject in itself. There can clearly be perversions and parasitic imitations, just as there can be over-intellectualised treatments of practices where the true significance is closely bound up with the figurative and symbolic expression. Symbolism is not a thing apart, a decorative superimposition: it is a major, and often indispensable way of articulating what is profoundly perceived and felt, and finds its appropriate depth in the fertilisation and sustaining of one another's experience within a continuing social unit. At the same time the symbol is not final, and the ritual must not become an end in itself, much less be exploited for purposes extrinsic to its proper motivation—indeed, as has sometimes happened, evil purposes.

All the same, in the last resort, the symbol is not final and it does not exist for itself. It derives its proper power from the continuity of the experience it expresses. The same is true in art. Poetry, or any other form of art, which depends entirely on lively image or emotional overtones is not the finest. It palls unless it high-lights or exhibits something distinctive and notable, however impossible it may be to distil the meaning from its figurative expression. The symbol must not, in religion, take wing on its own; it must be anchored in experience.

The same is true of the more formally credal expressions of religious truth. There is a place for sophisticated formulation, acutely difficult though it is and full of pitfalls, but it is not, as has alas too often been assumed, an *a priori* intellectual exercise. It proceeds on the basis of what is taken to be conveyed in the medium of live experiences enriching and extending one another in a variety of social contexts. This means that the theologian has a peculiarly difficult task and requires a greater variety of skills and aptitudes than is usually realised, least of all by the practitioners themselves—a point which I much stressed elsewhere.[5] It is particularly hard because one has to be responsive to the symbolism, and the appropriate artistry, and also to the critical assessment of all that these convey.

A very serious pitfall, most of all for Western theologians and religious thinkers, is to take some striking religious symbol or story out of its context in the total themes of the scriptures in which it appears. This has happened, for example, when juristic metaphors in the New Testament have been made the basis of doctrines of retributive punishment and vicarious suffering in ways appalling to any moral or intellectual sensitivity. Credal affirmations do have their important place, most of all in religions in which the historical factor is important. They help to concentrate attention in the right way. But they must proceed on the basis of what is initially made evident in the formative disclosures in experience.

In semitic religion there is usually accorded an exceptionally important place to a distinctive form which divine disclosure in human experience is alleged to have taken in a particular stretch of history. This is not the place to assess that claim, or the even more astounding claim that the one transcendent reality was able, in some way which baffles all comprehension, to so limit itself as to enter into a fully human limited form in the culmination of the process which had been taking shape in Hebrew history. This remains the central Christian affirmation and I myself make very little sense of recent attempts to retain the formulae and ritual practices of the Christian faith if these central themes, as they seem to me, of the New Testament and traditional Christian understanding are so eroded as to bear little relation to the sources from which they came and the meaning they would normally be given. Far better, it would seem to me, to abandon them altogether, though that is far from what I myself commend.

At the moment the question is not the soundness of the distinctive claims of the Christian faith or any other. But there is one point I do want to stress, namely that the assessment of these and like affirmations must, in the last analysis, go back to the profoundest appreciation of the subtle interlacing of normal sensitivity with divine intimation. If this adds up, in the available evidence about Jesus and his background, to the central affirmations of the New Testament and traditional Christian thought, so be it —it is what I myself think. But if the central claims are not to be sustained along those lines I know of no way in which they can be so sustained that can stand in the light of open reflection and criticism today.

It remains most important however to recognise that, whichever way the evidence points in respect to the distinctive stances of various religions, this is no bar to the profound recognition of one another's insights and achievements. We have learnt much better today how much of mutual enrichment of one another's experience and insight is possible in this way. The differences, where they remain, must not be blurred, any more than they must be hardened by misunderstanding. We can reach across to one another's practices and histories to the great deepening and enlivening of our own experiences, and the gain in this way to the West today is much too evident for me to need to underline it now. We have learnt enormously from varieties of experience that were new to us, and the range of our sensitivity has been much extended. Meditation has acquired a new depth for us, and flights of religious imagination opened up that were little known before. My contention is that the major clue for understanding and assessment, when expertise and scholarship has done its work, is the religious toning and directing of religious experience along the lines indicated.

There is one point of considerable substance which I would like to add. It refers to what I was saying at the beginning about the initial awareness of the transcendent. In my understanding, the transcendent is altogether beyond and other than finite being. Creaturely existence, though wholly dependent, is not any part or mode of ultimate being. This is however much in dispute, not only in extensive features of Eastern thought but in Western philosophies from Plotinus to Hegel and contemporary mystical philosophers like W. T. Stace. This again is a vast issue in itself and the opposition of view varies a great deal in its sharpness. I maintain, however, that this is the crucial issue for today in religious thought. It is not an easy one, and we all have our attachments to entrenched positions which we find hard to surrender. My own allegiance has been made plain in one publication after another. I strongly insist on the distinct reality of finite existence and especially on the peculiar distinctness of persons. On the line we take on this issue will turn, more than on anything else at present, the ultimate understanding we have, and even the sensitivity to genuine religious reality as such. It is an issue we must firmly face, though the last thing we must fall into is the temptation to settle the question lightly out of hand to ensure easy accommodation and good will. The right sort of good will does not call for that sort of price, and is contaminated by it. But we must have this central issue steadily before us, and it is on our success in coping with it, I maintain, that the best eventual progress will be made with all our other major problems and our power to share the wealth of one another's insights and experience.

I have spoken mainly of communication and assessment of truth. No space is left to consider the part which our own responsiveness plays in the process as a whole. The wind may blow 'where it listeth' but 'prayer and fasting' has its place too. An age committed to exclusively secular pursuits, and those not always the most elevated, can hardly expect to be well apprised of things that have to be 'spiritually discerned'. What Simone Weil and others have reminded us about heeding and 'waiting on God' is immensely relevant, and this means more than being religiously attentive in a general way: it means also the continual response, in practice as in thought, of individuals in the ebb and flow of the illumination they have in their own religious experience and what they assimilate from the religious life of their community. It is in these terms, in the exchanges of genuine response, in the part we play ourselves in the formulation of our own religious awareness, that we come again, if I may again reflect my personal allegiance, to our understanding of the more theistic approach to religion and our proper participation in it.

Religious experience, so conceived, is not passive, and it does not under-rate the essential mutuality of living personal relationship as involved centrally in it. The language of prayer and devotion, of struggle and surrender, as well as the essential serenity, bring us to the vitally personal character of religious existence which we are also apt to overlook, even though some like myself may be inclined to over-stress it. The 'God of the living', even of the wayward and rebellious, the relentlessly seeking God, is the God I have encountered in my own experience.

I hope such an element of personal testimony is not out of place. What matters for us here is that, in discussion and amity, we should enter into one another's views and sensitivity with as much imaginative insight and empathy as we can. Where the gaps can be closed let us hasten to do so, but our main concern is with the truth and 'the wind of the argument whithersoever it takes us'. We must understand as much as we can across the boundaries, with humility as much as with firmness. There is no place in true religion for confrontation or rancour; there is all the place in the world for empathy and humility.

NOTES

1. Hywel D. Lewis, *Our Experience of God* (London: Allen & Unwin, 1959). Cf. also Chap. iii of my *Persons and Life After Death* (London: Macmillan, 1978).
2. Alasdair MacIntyre and Anthony Flew (eds.), *New Essays in Philosophical Theology*, Chap. xiv (London: SCM Press, 1955).
3. Hywel D. Lewis, *The Elusive Mind* (London: Allen & Unwin, 1969).
4. F. Sontag, *Divine Perfection* (London: Student Movement Press, 1962).
5. Hywel D. Lewis, 'What is Theology?', *Freedom and History*, Chap. xvii (London: Allen & Unwin, 1962).

2 Christology and Prevarication

Traditionally, the Christian faith has accorded a central role to Jesus, not merely in the form of the reverence due to the founder of a great movement, but as the person around whom it all revolves. This has also normally involved the extraordinary claim that Jesus, while fully human in all ways as we are, is also God, or, more ambiguously, that we reaffirm the divinity of Jesus. Theological controversy has centred largely on the way to sustain this affirmation and on the implications it has 'for us and our salvation', in the familiar words. There is no need to review the familiar answers here, sometimes sacrificing the humanity to the divinity, and sometimes the reverse. In our time there has been little inclination to question the full humanity of Jesus, on occasion laying emphasis upon it beyond obvious need. To question it would seem to most intellectually responsible religious people to undermine both the relevance and the credibility of the Christian religion. Nothing must be done to impair the full humanity of Jesus in every way. On this many voices are raised, and that is no doubt a salutary thing and a welcome feature of religious life today. Its ramifications are many. But this only sharpens the question of the traditional allegation of the divinity of Jesus, and on this there are many discordant voices, including those which firmly repudiate this term of the traditional paradox.

There are two ways in which the divinity of Jesus may be firmly repudiated by persons who would still wish to regard themselves and be described as Christians, followers of Christ. The first, and more questionable one, is that of one form of Christian humanism. The latter term has many applications, and it can be very properly used to describe those thinkers, like More and Erasmus, who, from the centre of the main stream of Christian affirmation, have laid special emphasis on the reasonableness of faith and the importance of human aptitudes and responsibility. But I use the term 'humanism' now in the way that is most usual today to indicate a strictly secular attitude in which no reference is made to anything not comprehensible entirely in terms of the needs and aspirations and attitudes of men as they find themselves in the present existence. Can we sensibly speak of a Christian form of this humanism?

I do not think we can rule that out, although we need also to be very careful here not to prevaricate, or to countenance and encourage prevarication. Provided the sort of humanism under consideration now is explicit and clear about its intentions, there is no reason why it should not draw much of its inspiration and momentum from the teaching and example of Jesus, or indeed regard Jesus, if it wishes, as the pre-eminent example and source of the kind of humanism it wishes to further and practise. But it must do this warily if it is not to find itself involved in practices and attitudes of mind which cannot be effectively dissociated from assumptions and sentiments expressive of the underlying themes of main-stream Christianity. This is peculiarly so if more is retained than admiring intellectual acknowledgement of any preeminence accorded to the insights and sensitivity of Jesus on the moral and social matters that concern us here and now.

A sensitive secular humanist may be very tender in his regard for Jesus, and why not? On any count it would be difficult to find greater human insight, or more penetrating involvement in the more sensitive areas of human relations, than in the teaching and example of Jesus. We must not deny him to those who do not come further with us along the way, and if we were to do so that would be a very poor service to the proper understanding of him and the eventual appreciation of the deeper allegiance we think we should also have. Many fine secular humanists have a better claim to be 'in the Kingdom' than many other 'practising' Christians. He (Jesus) would not deny them and it is not for us to take away their Lord.

But we have also to be careful and clear-sighted. The secular humanist must not go too far, nor presume too much, in adaptations of traditional ritual and sentiments for the cultivation and dynamism of his own commitment. If he does so he may confuse both himself and others. If there is a bleakness in his attitudes which he finds it hard to endure, he must learn to live with it; he must not warm himself at the fire of a faith he does not hold.

I had occasion many years ago[1] to refer to the suggestion of the Freudian psychologist, J. C. Flugel, that 'religious emotions must be largely or entirely secularized and be put in the service of humanity'.[2] This has obvious attractions for one who believes that 'the religion of humanity is surely the religion of the nearer future'.[3] If religion is defunct the dynamism of it, and the power of its symbolism, may be put to other use. We must redeem what we can. Flugel is at least clear-sighted. So is another psychologist, Eric Fromm, who is adept at baptising religious language into a secular use. On the other hand I stand by the warning I issued earlier. The dynamism of religious language and emotions may not retain much of its potency in another setting; it will be too much diluted without the faith which prompted it. In the meantime there can be engendered much confusion about the stances of people who retain religious terms and symbolism in a fully secular context; and the proper understanding and appraisal of religious notions may be seriously frustrated in the ambiguities of non-religious extensions of the terms and attitudes by which they are normally expressed. Is it enough to be clear-sighted, and how many remain, in the present practice, as clear-sighted as Flugel or Fromm?

A peculiarly intriguing example for us to note here is that of Iris Murdoch whose very remarkable novels are redolent of religious themes and nuances. To learn about lostness in the world of today, in a properly religious or in a secular sense, we can do much worse than read these books—'they seemed to have been alone, really related to each other at last, in an awful shut-in solitude, becoming demons to each other.'[4] The return from fantasy to realism, and the healing function of art in this redeeming activity, is peculiarly well presented: 'It's as if I'd been, all the time, looking into a mirror, and only been vaguely conscious of the real world at my side.'[5] Even the description, simple but rendered all the more alarming by the absence of artificial embellishments, of the two people trapped in a cave (in *The Nice and the Good*) has an unmistakable religious nuance. So has the extensive concern with guilt and evil, compassion and transfiguration and healing; and it is plain that all these, as in much else in remarkable contemporary fiction if we heeded it more, are extremely revealing in the properly religious way. The intention all the same is severely secular, notwithstanding the dim religious light in which it is placed. Perhaps it is only in that context that religious significance may be recovered. But we have to take the subtleties and complexities of these situations further to find their proper religious import; and without that there may be much distortion and a return to that very world of today which the author rightly dreads.

This becomes peculiarly evident when Miss Murdoch presents her own views, not in the wide range and allusiveness of fiction, but more overtly in her lectures, *The Sovereignty of Good*.[6] On religion, as normally understood, her views are quite explicit. She says:

> We are what we seem to be, transient mortal creatures subject to necessity and chance. This is to say that there is, in my view, no God in the traditional sense of that term; and the traditional sense is perhaps the only sense. When Bonhoeffer says that God wants us to live as if there were no God I suspect he is misusing words. Equally the various metaphysical substitutes for God— Reason, Science, History—are false deities. Our destiny can be examined but it cannot be justified or totally explained. We are simply here. And if there is any kind

of sense or unity in human life, and the dream of this does not cease to haunt us, it is of some other kind and must be sought within a human experience which has nothing outside it. (p. 79)

'There is no God.' But what then becomes of prayer and sacrament and other 'techniques of religion', (p. 55) and of all the talk of original sin and of fallen man? (p. 51). For the latter we may take our cue from Freud. The rest seems to call for some kind of transcendent. But it is an entirely ethical transcendent and containable therefore 'within a human experience which has nothing outside it' (p. 79). 'I shall suggest that God was (or is) a *single perfect transcendent non-representable and necessarily real object of attention*; and I shall go on to suggest that moral philosophy should attempt to retain a central concept which has all these characteristics' (p. 55). The attempt to provide this kind of moral philosophy has many points of interest. Orientation is stressed and 'the quality of habitual objects of attention'. 'We can all receive moral help by focusing our attention upon things which are valuable' (p. 56). The order of the virtues is stressed and the way that reflection 'tends to unify the moral world' (p. 57). Above all we must avoid personal fantasy, 'the chief enemy of excellence in morality'. The 'reflection of the real world' must not be dimmed 'by assertion of self' (p. 59). This is where we find the great therapeutic value of art, which helps us to pierce the veil of selfish consciousness and join the world as it really is. It leads to acceptance of death as 'the acceptance of our own nothingness which is an automatic spur to our own concern with what is not ourselves' (p. 103). There is a detachment which enables us to look at the world as it really is, to have 'respect for the real' and 'keep the attention fixed upon the real situation', and in this way 'In intellectual discipline and in the enjoyment of art and nature we discover value in our ability to forget self, to be realistic, to perceive justly' (p. 90). We avoid the false 'consolations of self-pity, resentment, fantasy and despair' (p. 91). There is 'pure delight in the independent existence of what is excellent' (p. 85).

It is in this way that we acquire 'The image of the Good as a transcendent magnetic centre' (p. 75). This 'Good is still somewhere beyond' and this gives us what we need as 'the non-metaphysical meaning of the idea of transcendence' (p. 93), and in this context we can also see how the believer 'needs, and can receive, extra help'. 'Not I, but Christ' (p. 83). But this must not be 'used as an argument for the truth of religious doctrines' (p. 83). It refers to the right sort of 'supplemental energy' which comes from getting beyond the 'falsifying veil' and looking at the world as it really is. I am 'brooding perhaps on some damage done to my prestige. Then suddenly I observe a hovering kestrel. In a moment everything is altered. The brooding self with its hurt vanity has disappeared' (p. 84).

There is much in this to which we can readily respond. The sort of detachment described here is of great importance, and it is a basic ingredient in religion and the religious apprehension of truth. In the details, the interpretation of Kant for example and some references to contemporary philosophers, we may have much to quarrel with. But the stress on the importance of being open to the real impact of the world upon us, and the place of art in maintaining this, should be most welcome in religious thought at present. But it falls very far short all the same of the fullness of transcendence in the proper religious sense. It is certainly not the case, as Miss Murdoch seems to imply, that it was in her sense that Plato found the Good to be 'beyond being and knowledge' and I do not think the 'Mystics of all kinds' would settle, as she also contends, for her sense of 'the nakedness and aloneness of Good, its absolute for-nothingness' (p. 42). What she does, in some ways with great sensitivity, is to high-light some of the things most distinctive and profound in genuine religion and baptise them into much curtailed versions of themselves. She has no illusions about this, and that is peculiarly welcome at present. What she says is illuminating for our understanding of religion. But we would be badly wrong in supposing that she begins to get to the heart of what has appeared to be of most importance in religion as we normally think of it.

This can be said of those religions, of which Buddhism is the obvious example, which appear not to venture much beyond the ground mapped out by Miss Murdoch. For even here, at the centre of what appears to be a firm rejection of all metaphysics, there is much that does not come properly within the compass of 'human experience which has nothing outside it' (p. 79). The reference to a metaphysical transcendent, a genuine reality 'beyond', is not just cautious in Miss Murdoch's work, it is altogether absent, and quite intentionally so. Whatever mystery means, it is not that which usually moves and over-whelms the religious devotee. She may share some of his insights and use his language, but she does not begin to approach the 'Idea of the Holy'; and of this she is fully, and most commendably, aware herself.

I have been noting examples of attempts to adapt some of the themes, and the language and symbolism, of traditional religion, and especially here Christian theism, without any concern to retain 'the old concept of God' even 'in a thin disguise', or reach in any other way beyond the human situation. This has the important merit of clarity, and whatever it borrows is acknowledged and made to stand firmly on its own in the new context.

I move now to a further way in which the alleged divinity of Jesus would be firmly and unambiguously repudiated by persons who would also claim close affinity with him; and here we shall find ourselves moving close again to the traditional fold. I refer to the unitarians. Their view is in no way a secular one. They acknowledge and worship the same God as other Christians. Nor do they think—at least not usually—of this God in a remote and deistic way. They can, and usually do, endorse all that is traditionally said about the disclosure of God in history and human experience. They acknowledge that God has spoken in diverse times and places, and that he speaks with intimacy as 'a God of the living' coming to terms with our situation and our waywardness. All that Christians traditionally say in this vein the unitarian can endorse (he is not bound to be a deist), and there have been some

notable unitarian leaders and thinkers who have done
much to advance and to deepen Christian understanding.
A notable recent example would be the late Dr A. C.
Ewing[7] whose splendid contribution to religious thought
today we underestimate at our peril.

It is not out of the question, it would not even seem
strange, for the unitarian to affirm that 'God was in Christ
reconciling the world to himself'. But he would understand this without any recourse to any divine role which
was an essential feature of the work of Christ. The main
inspiration of his life would be found in the life and
teaching of Jesus. It is, in this way, that he finds himself in
Jesus closest to God. There is more of God in Jesus, he
might put it, than anywhere else. He will speak with
reverence of Jesus as the most inspiring religious figure he
knows, and he may go further and say that he does not
expect to find this ever excelled. In this and related ways
he can come close to other Christians in worship and
practice and join in saying many of the things they say. In
much of his demeanour as a Christian there may not be
much to choose between him and others.

All the same there will be a radical difference, and it is
an outstanding merit of the unitarian position as a rule to
be quite clear-sighted about it. The difference is that the
unitarian makes no claim to interpret his devotion or
loyalty to Christ, or any basis he has for this, in terms of
any status to be accorded to Jesus beyond a fine but
exclusively human one. However much we may say that
God was pre-eminently in him we do not, on unitarian
views, understand this as radically different, even if it
involves some special finality and completeness (which is
not the case for all unitarians), from the involvement of
God in other human lives, in saints and prophets and
other profoundly spiritual people, or perhaps as disclosed
in some measure in everyone. There are many types of
unitarianism, some closer to traditional Christianity than
others, some inclining more to the views of secular
humanists, but they all have one thing in common—and
this is what is meant by the term 'unitarian'—namely that
they repudiate any strict identification of Jesus with God

or the view that God could so limit himself as actually, without ceasing to be God, to be also a fully limited human being. The traditional paradox does not trouble them, for they firmly, and without any ambiguity, repudiate the most bewildering term of it.

It is for this reason that unitarians are careful, as a rule, to ensure that any metaphorical or symbolical terms they use, however important for worship and commendation, are not of the kind which would seriously lead to the ascription of divinity to Jesus. This is not just a question of trinitarian doctrine or whether we should seriously speak of three persons in the Godhead. It is more basic than that, namely the firm repudiation of the divinity of Jesus, irrespective of the way this may be further conceived and formulated in theological doctrine. Nothing is to be claimed about Jesus which could not in principle be said about other finite creatures. He is part of God's creation, not one with the Creator. On this there is nothing to choose between the unitarian view and that of Islam. In Muslim teaching it is sheer idolatry to regard any man, however fine, as being 'in the form of God' or 'equal with God'.[8] Christian unitarians may not, in the case of Jesus, share the Muslim's abhorrence of the impugning of the majesty of God in the ascription of divinity to Jesus, but in essentials their view is the same.

I have spoken at some length about the unitarian position because, in the context of the rejection of the alleged divinity of Jesus, it has the important merit, already noted, of being explicit and without prevarication. This, as we shall see, is to be sharply contrasted with the attitudes of many writers of today who seem to share the convictions of the unitarians without their clarity or their boldness in dispensing with the support and conveniences of a position they do not seriously hold. I shall return to this theme, but in the meantime I wish first to refer to other notable views which have much in common with unitarian teaching.

The most important of these are found in post-Hegelian idealism. The essence of this teaching is that the entire universe is one all-inclusive system; there is no ultimate distinctness of things or persons. Everything is some part, or more strictly an appearance or manifestation, of the one whole. There are finite centres of this whole, at least in some versions of this view, but their true reality is in their place in the whole. The whole pervades and dominates everything. The problems which all this presents are familiar and need not be rehearsed here — they are especially acute in respect to freedom and evil. But the idealist metaphysical monism does allow one way in which it is plausible to speak of the divinity of Jesus without the usual complications and problems of a more strict and orthodox Christology.

This is because we can sensibly say, in idealist terms, that there is some measure of divinity in all of us, not in the subdued sense of being made in the image of God, but in the firmer sense that we all partake in some measure in the one reality of the whole, the absolute, whether or not we call it God. The whole, or God, as some idealists[9] explicitly call it, reflects itself more completely in some than in others, and in some it does this superbly. In Jesus, it could be thus argued, the divine shines with a special radiance or with a finality not elsewhere found in finite existence.[10] It was along these lines that one influential idealist teacher, in the heyday of this movement, replied to a colleague who taxed him on his having allegedly denied the divinity of Jesus: 'I have not denied the divinity of any man.' This was a clever riposte, and perfectly in order for an idealist philosopher, but it is also very far removed from the intentions of traditional Christology. The divinity of Jesus is not, in orthodox teaching, a matter of degree or something which could be claimed in some measure for all. There is a very strict identity.

Orthodox Christian teaching would also be much out of accord with the monism of idealist philosophy. God, in normal Christian teaching, in itself and in its background, is distinct from his creation, the author and sustainer of all, infinite and unconditioned by contrast with all other limited and conditioned existences. He is transcendent, in the strictest sense and, in this at least, 'wholly other' and distinct. This makes it harder, in some respects at least, to present an acceptable Christology, but it was on this basis that the main Christian tradition claimed a unique once for all incarnation of God in Jesus—and in no other.

The idealist view has much in common with some forms of Oriental metaphysics and religion, notably some versions of Hinduism, and the rapprochement between Hinduism and idealist philosophy—still widely acclaimed in India—was very close at one time. This was one way in which the idea of the avatar would be understood. But there are other more total and mystical forms of monism in which finite existence disappears more completely or is recognised solely as illusion. The one reality is the self, and the self in all is the same. This also gives us a sense in which there is 'a spark of the divine' in us all. But this is still further removed from Christian metaphysics and the claim that God was incarnate once for all in one fully real human person.

With the demise of idealism there was, on the continent of Europe, by contrast with the Anglo-Saxon empiricist and linguistic reaction, a sharp swing back to very firm and assertive transcendentalist theology, notably that of Barth. This was also a return to orthodoxy, but in a curious form. The emphasis on the transcendent, and the rejection of rather facile accounts of religious realities in so-called Liberal theology, led to what some have named 'The Religious Revolt against Reason'.[11] If God was 'wholly other' or beyond, there was no way in which he could be comprehended in rational terms, or his dealings with us explained. This was a reaction we can understand, but, as I maintained in much of my earlier work, it led to very deplorable obscurantism. The stress on the transcendent does not warrant unreason or any irresponsible thinking, but so long as this kind of theology was in vogue, there could not be much encouragement to attempts to provide any acceptable basis or justification for incarnational doctrine. We had to make do with either doctrinal or Biblical fundamentalism, usually the former with powerful insistence on the Bible as its basis. The stricter doctrine of the Incarnation came thus to be reaffirmed, as a vital part of orthodox teaching, but without the recognition of any need for a properly rational and ascertainable basis on which it could be commended.

This went along with, and deepened, an extensive, almost militant, scepticism about the historicity of the vital Biblical documents, especially the gospels. This was not thought to be a worry, for the tradition was to draw its strength from the way the Word of God became directly meaningful and authoritative for those who turned properly to it. Historical scepticism was no obstacle to traditional orthodoxy; on the contrary it strengthened it, and the deeper this kind of scepticism the profounder and firmer was our hold on the truth now being properly apprehended.

This story comes to its culmination with the intrusion into historical scepticism, in combination with strong doctrinal dogmatism, of recent philosophical scepticism and especially the combination of allegedly Wittgensteinian philosophy with religious fideism, of which it is by no means certain that Wittgenstein himself would have approved. Wittgenstein wrote little about religion and it is by no means easy to determine what, if anything, he thought about it. The most that we can elicit from him, it seems to me, is a general caution about anything we venture to say about such elusive topics as the soul or God, and this, while obviously not so astoundingly new, is sensible enough as far as it goes. But in some quarters it is taken as a cue to proceed to practise most that we normally do in various religions, or forms of these religions, without much in the way of the credal affirmations that would normally be taken to warrant those practices or things said in a ritual way, or indeed any clearly ascertainable belief at all.

This approach to religion has been the subject of extensive comment and this is not the place to add to what I and others have said about it elsewhere. The main difficulty is to know what it is with which we have to come to grips, the language of religion being wholly divorced from the ordinary meaning of words, a world, or a 'game' (sic), with rules, if there are any, altogether peculiar to itself. From the proper insistence that what we say in prayer or sacrament or in talk about life after death is not altogether in line with similar things that we say in day-to-day concerns, the strange conclusion seems to be drawn that there is no way in which the meaning of what we say can be noted and considered other than in our indulgence in the practices themselves and their context. In these terms it is very hard to avoid an outright relativism where there can be no reason for preferring enlightened religious views, as they would normally be thought to be, to the most savage and barbarous religious practices: the 'game' is played in each case and there are no rules which it does not posit itself. The door is wide open, and the excesses and perversities of the 'new religions', as they are sometimes called, have as rightful a place in our esteem as the most high-minded and reflective Christian practice. The drift towards a vague secularism is also very marked.

When I contemplate this kind of fideism, and the vast amount of perplexing literature which it seems to be spawning, I am inclined to call to mind a visit to an aviary near my home, 'the Bird-World', which I made recently with an American friend I was entertaining. In one corner there were some magnificent owls, and we very much admired one brown owl. It stood firmly on its perch, its head a little sunk in its neck, the embodiment of profundity and wisdom. From time to time it swivelled its head round, with just one eye open and that inclined to wink a little. Under the penetration of its glance, from within the remoteness in which it was wrapped, everything seemed to dwindle into insignificance or shame; and there, it seemed to me, go the new Wittgensteinians, looking round from the secure perch of their own noncommitment and silence with an air designed to make everything we venture upon appear trivial and naive, but themselves saying nothing beyond the same monotonous tu-whit tu-who in answer to all problems.

It is in this welter of confusion that we must place the ambiguities of the new Christologies. There must, it appears, be no proper abandonment of the form of

Christological faith and confession, for the price would be very high. So something must be retained, if only a form of words, without any of the substance of what would normally be understood by talk of the divinity of Jesus or of his being also Christ. The idea that God was incarnate in a particular person must not be thrown overboard, but it must be re-interpreted in a way that does not present any of the traditional problems or impose any strain on our faith and understanding. The convenient word 'myth' is made to work over-time for this purpose.

It is in this vein, so it seems to me, that Professor Ninian Smart writes as follows in the chapter on Christianity in his book *Background to the Long Search*[12] designed to provide appropriate information and background for viewers of a televised programme on world religions:

> Probably every image has a certain truth. But we soon see that it is not sensible to look on Jesus in just one way. All the search-lights we illuminate him with have differently coloured beams. So what is the point of asking what his real colour is.

He adds:

> And of course whether Jesus is saviour is not so much a matter of history as of sacred drama or (to use another term) myth.

There is much here that calls for comment, the implicit relativism, for example. We do disagree about a great many things, both trivial and important, and we look upon them differently. But it does not follow that the truth itself varies in the same way, or that we may not have very good grounds for our confidence that we have it in some matters. It is just possible that I am wrong in thinking that it is raining now, but when I have looked out of the window I have no serious doubts about it. Nor is disagreement a proper reason for scepticism or relativism. No one is infallible, and we should hold our views, even on the matters of most importance for us, with openness and respect for the views of others. But this is perfectly compatible with strong and sensibly held conviction. Indeed, the stronger our convictions the less are we inclined to repudiate the objectivity of the claim to truth. The soldier and the pacifist disagree on matters of life and death, but the one, in respecting the sincerity of the other, does not just shrug his shoulders and declare that they must both be right. On the contrary they are very eager to convince one another of the soundness of their respective opinions.

This is very evident in day-to-day matters. If my friend assures me that it is noon when I think it is 11 a.m., we both wonder whose watch has stopped or run ahead, or look for some like solution. We cannot both be right, but there is a true and false to what we think, and the proper course is to renew our efforts to learn properly what is the case. Similarly in science. Outstanding scientists some-times disagree, as in the recent debate between Martin Ryle and Fred Hoyle. But this only sharpens their deter-mination to settle the issue one way or the other, by finding new evidence or a better way of understanding the evidence available. In ethics, as was made evident by a group of impressive thinkers earlier this century, Moore, Broad, Ross, Ewing and others, the way we hold our opinions, even when they differ very sharply, in-volves the conviction that there is a truth for us to strive after, and ways of making it more likely that we have attained it. Truth is not easy of attainment in religion, but that is no reason for despair or scepticism. We do indeed hold different views about Jesus, but that does not mean that we need not continue the effort to have a sound view of him.

It is not clear to me how we are to understand the notions of 'sacred drama' or 'myth' as presented by Professor Smart. To say that something is a myth, in common parlance today, is usually to dismiss it or at least to disavow any claim to truth in respect of it. Professor Smart does not, presumably, wish to take that line. If the drama is sacred it is clearly important. But is it important as something we take to be the case? The historicity at least does not seem to matter much for Professor Smart. The truth of the myth, if truth is claimed for it, must be sought mainly elsewhere; and in one respect at least this is sound. We cannot settle a religious issue on mere empirical evidence about the past; evaluation and religious discernment come in. But it does not follow that we cannot have a reasonable view of figures of note in religion, and that what we believe in this historical way is not vital. To speak of sacred drama leaves it very open what sort of claim to truth is being made.

The idea of myth has, however, a very strong appeal to religious thinkers today. If it merely means that we must not take everything at its face value, or that we often have to use symbolical terms for which, in some contexts at least, there may be no substitute, the point can be readily conceded. 'Symbolism and belief' is a very central theme in religious thinking, today as in the past. This makes questions of true and false harder, but it does not enable us to push the claim to truth off the stage. Nor is it implied, in the symbolic character of religious utterances, that we can interpret or reduce them in any way we please. The general implication of much recent talk about myth, in religious contexts, has been, however, in respect of the idea of incarnation especially, that transformations are in order which take us away altogether from the initial and normal meaning of terms. If, as I have stressed, this is openly done, the mischief is at least contained. It is a very different matter when the aura of some special sanctity, or nuances appropriate only to claims to be understood in one particular way, are retained in contexts where they are no longer significant.

This, it seems to me, is just what has happened in much of the recent talk about the 'myth of God incarnate'. That the incarnation is in some respects irreducibly mysterious is clear, and we did not have to wait for contemporary insights to appreciate this. We may seriously mishandle it if we fail to realise how subtle and difficult to apprehend properly it is, or if we treat it with a crude literalness. There is a great deal that needs qualification when we speak of God 'being made man'. But under cover of this very necessary caution we must not go to the other extreme of supposing that no literal element at all is involved. The latter error is what seems to me to characterise much recent theological thinking.

Nowhere is this more evident than in the much publicised book of that title, *The Myth of God Incarnate*.[13] This book has already received wide attention, perhaps more than it deserves, and it would be tedious to go again over the very familiar ground of objections and counter-objections to this book. But it has some features which it may be worth noting here before we pass to more impressive presentations of the same themes. One is that already noted, namely the ambiguity of retaining suggestions and nuances of more than the situation warrants. The other, not so much remarked upon, is to divert attention, though not of set purpose to mislead, from the extent of the Copernican revolution proposed, and its gravity, by presenting the alternatives to it in crudely simplistic terms which few of those who wish to adhere to a more traditional view would wish to endorse or to countenance at all.

It would take much space to illustrate this in detail and set us covering ground too familiar for me to detain you on it. I will therefore simply refer at this stage to one of the papers and some points made in it which are peculiarly revealing for the very heart of the enterprise undertaken. I refer to the paper by Dr Michael Goulder entitled 'Jesus, The Man of Universal Destiny'.[14]

There arises from time to time, Dr Goulder holds, a man of destiny, the ground-swell of history bringing on a crisis which produces 'a leader who expresses in his whole personality the community and movement of which he is a part'. 'Such were Themistocles, Joan of Arc, Churchill.' 'The hour is at hand when the issue must be decided',[15] political freedom being a prominent part of the main aspiration. 'It was a very strong element with Gandhi and Luther King.'[16] But Jesus was different from most of these—'he was a man of universal destiny'. But he was 'not just one of a group of men of universal destiny, with Mohammed, Gautama Buddha, etc.: he is *the* man of universal destiny', having the role, as 'destined by God', 'to establish the community of selfless love in the world'.[17]

It is admitted that a humanist would find much of this acceptable. 'Humanists also believe in the primacy of love',[18] and a humanist might 'see and admire Jesus as the prime historical source for the first full teaching of love, and its realisation in an ongoing human community'.[19] But Dr Goulder is not, he assures us, however, a humanist. He goes further, in the insistence that it was God who had destined Jesus in this way. 'Jesus' life was God's master-stroke. When the fullness of time had come, God revealed to Jesus his destiny; and Jesus was obedient, even unto the death of the cross—that is, he responded day by day to the ever-broadening vision of what this destiny was to demand of him.'[20]

There is every justification for the claim that this takes us beyond secular humanism. But how far beyond it does it go? It accords a unique role to Jesus, and one for which he was especially destined by God. But the unitarians whom I mentioned earlier would happily go the whole way with Dr Goulder here. Is that where he stands? If so, it would help to make that more explicit. The label may not be a very elegant one, and it is none of my concern to persuade Dr Goulder or any others to carry a particular name. But it is important that the affinity should be made quite explicit, and what I detect, even more markedly elsewhere in the book, is that the authors, not surprisingly in view of the high ecclesiastical offices that many of them hold, are haunted by the need to reflect, in however tentative a fashion, some further plus of significance more in line with the traditional confession of Christian faith. Is their revolution as complete as, in consistency, it should be?

My second point is well illustrated in the sort of things, more than anything else, which Dr Goulder thinks he is leaving behind him—'the endless round of empty speculations that run from the implausible to the irreligious: the theories that point to demons more powerful than God (unless he can cheat them), and those that posit a faceless justice more powerful than God; those that make Christ a whipping boy, and those that make him an international banker in merit, with resources enough to pay off the world's balance of payments deficit'—'rubbish, added to rubbish'.[21] There have no doubt been versions, in the long course of Christian thinking, of the notions mocked here, and they deserve the castigation they get. It is well to remember, at the same time, that here also we must not take everything at its face value, least of all when we come across notions of this kind in poetical or imaginative parts of sacred writings. What a hymn says, for example, it says as a wholeness of its rhythm and music and overt meaning together. But this is a theme in itself. I fully endorse, as will most Christian thinkers today, the condemnation of the appalling suppositions to which Dr Goulder refers. How far they have in fact been held may not be as easy to settle as might be thought. But they, and their like, have undoubtedly been a strain and an embarrassment in Christian witness.

I have in fact been myself as contentious a critic of some of the travesties, as they seem to me, of Christian truth as any, and have myself been reprobated in turn for my much too Liberal approach to Christian themes. It is not, I hope, improper to mention, in the context of my strictures on Dr Goulder's views, my own earlier books, *Morals and the New Theology*[22] and *Morals and Revelation*.[23] But however readily we agree with Dr Goulder here, it would be quite wrong to conclude that the role accorded to Jesus in the main tradition, and his status in his special oneness with God, were invented to provide a foundation for objectionable speculation and doctrines such as those which shock Dr Goulder. The initial claim made about Jesus came about, on the contrary, in the immediate impact he made. Many factors besides this entered into the subsequent development of Christian doctrines, and they included, as I have stressed elsewhere, various shifts to soften the rigour of the demands of Christian discipleship upon us. Perhaps it is to that source, more than anything, that we must trace the more distressing aberrations of traditional doctrine. But even those, we must not forget, however distorted, rested on a core of initial apprehension which the subsequent distortion did nothing to impair.

It should be added, in some extenuation of the mistakes of the past, that any matters affecting the ultimate dealing of God with man are peculiarly difficult to handle, and, for this reason, the cruder sorts of short-circuiting would present a standing temptation—the pitfalls are many, and, once we are in, it is by no means easy to climb out of them: one misrepresentation calls for another in a mounting scandal. It is a moot point, however, how persistent, and how serious in their impact on Christian consciousness, were the suppositions which we find peculiarly repugnant. I suspect that many good Christians took them in their stride although that is not a very healthy situation to have to be in. In the main they were subdued, and some at least of the sting was taken out of them, in sincere Christian piety, by a deep and moving sense of the wonder of 'the Person'.

The procedure of Dr Goulder, in the present matter, smacks to me very much of the way Bertrand Russell or Bernard Shaw set up Christian men of straw at whom to shoot the barbs of their simplistic wit and mockery. I do not think many Christians, at any time, have believed the sort of things which Russell set up as a target for his criticisms in *Why I am not a Christian*; and if they did it was with qualifications of which no account was taken. There was no probing to find what moved people to seem to commit themselves to simple-minded and scandalous utterance. I think Dr Goulder might have probed further also—after all does not he himself mention 'the price of sin' which 'no other was good enough to pay' but Jesus and remind us that 'By his stripes we are healed'?[24]

To conclude, it is not to the travesties and aberrations that we must look for the proper alternative to Dr Goulder's own proposals. To censure the aberrations is not enough. We must go back to consider more carefully what is of greatest relevance to us today in the deep and rich deposit of Christian belief and witness in the past. But the proposals advanced in books like *The Myth of God Incarnate* have been presented in a more sustained and careful way, sometimes by the same authors, in more substantial studies by some highly placed and influential theologians of today. It will be well to look at samples of their work, and it is to this that I now turn.

NOTES

1. Hywel D. Lewis, *Our Experience of God* (London: Allen & Unwin, 1959) pp. 97–8.
2. J. C. Flugel, *Man, Morals and Society* (London: Duckworth & Co., 1948) p. 275.
3. Ibid., p. 275.
4. Iris Murdoch, *Bruno's Dream* (London: Chatto & Windus, 1969) p. 13.
5. Iris Murdoch, *The Unicorn* (New York: Viking Press, 1963) p. 208.
6. Iris Murdoch, *The Sovereignty of Good* (London: Routledge & Kegan Paul, 1970). Page numbers in brackets refer to this book.
7. See especially Dr A. C. Ewing's *Value and Reality* (London: Allen & Unwin, 1973).
8. Philippians 2, 6.
9. G. F. Stout, for example, in *God and Nature* (Cambridge University Press, 1962).
10. An excellent exposition of this view by a leading idealist writer of our times is found in *Atheism and Theism* by Errol E. Harris (New Orleans: Tulane University, 1977). For a splendid review of this book see *Religious Studies* Dec. 1979.
11. See especially Professor Harold de Wolff's book of that title—*The Religious Revolt against Reason* (New York: Harper Brothers, 1949).
12. Ninian Smart, *Background to the Long Search* (London: BBC Publications, 1977) p. 109.
13. John Hick (ed.), *The Myth of God Incarnate* (London: SCM Press, 1977).
14. Michael Goulder, 'Jesus, The Man of Universal Destiny' in *The Myth of God Incarnate*, John Hick (ed.) (London: SCM Press, 1977).
15. Ibid., pp. 55 and 56.
16. Ibid., p. 56.
17. Ibid., pp. 57 and 60.
18. Ibid., p. 60.
19. Ibid., p. 60.
20. Ibid., p. 61.
21. Ibid., p. 58.
22. Hywel D. Lewis, *Morals and the New Theology* (London: Victor Gollancz, 1947).
23. Hywel D. Lewis, *Morals and Revelation* (London: Allen & Unwin, 1951).
24. Michael Goulder, op. cit. p. 58.

3 'The Christ Event'

I would like to begin at this point by considering the peculiar, but for many people intriguing, procedures of Professor Maurice Wiles, Canon of Christ Church, Oxford. In his article 'Does Christology rest on a mistake?'[1] he begins with a very close parallel which he draws between the idea of the incarnation and the ideas of creation and the Fall. No intelligent person thinks today of creation in a literal way along the lines of the Book of Genesis—it was not a once-for-all event a few thousand years ago. It is a continuing process of sustaining the contingent finite universe in a way which goes beyond all but the dimmest understanding on our part. God did not create the world as we make things. Nor is creative activity restricted or manifested only in special events or parts of the universe, though there may well be events which make us appreciate better than others that the world is created. The divine creativity is everywhere.

Likewise, the doctrine of the Fall does not refer to the wrong choice taken by one individual in the garden of Eden. It refers to something, a 'fallen state' as some would put it, which is true of us all. There is no problem, for enlightened persons today, of 'the historicity of Adam's primordial transgression'.[2] We do not think in those terms any longer.

Why not, then, make a like adaptation of the idea of the incarnation in line with the way we think about these things today? The 'doctrine of creation does *not* require the postulation of any specific divine act within the process as a whole; indeed such an act would be an embarrassment to the expression of that doctrine in its full transcendent reality. Can we not say the same of the doctrine of redemption? Is it perhaps possible that the truth of that doctrine would even stand out more clearly if it were not tied to one particular act or life differing in kind from the rest of the series of human acts and human lives?'[3] The radical 'mistake' on which traditional theology 'rests' came about because 'the person and act of the redeemer were understood to be divine in a direct and special sense'.[4]

Originally, 'the theological conviction of the reality of divine redemption was felt to require the underpinning of a distinct divine presence in Jesus'.[5] We do not now require this, although there is some 'specialness of Jesus'. 'In other words, the story of Jesus is not an arbitrarily chosen story; from a Christian standpoint, it is the story of that historical happening which did in fact create a new and effective realization of divine redemption at work in the lives of men, and which has remained the inspirational centre of the community of faith to which we belong from that day until now'.[6]

Professor Wiles notes that, in presenting this claim, most of all 'in an inter-religious context', we reach a point where we can only say 'I can give no further reasons for seeing the thing as I do; this is my vision; do you not feel drawn to share it too?'[7] I am much in sympathy with this, and I also have stressed (especially in my 'Ultimates and a way of looking' in my *Persons and Life after Death*)[8] that we are bound to reach a point, in all our thinking, where we can only say how things seem to us to be, though not, as must also be stressed, with any impairment of objectivity. The claim is about what is really the case. But where this is invoked by Professor Wiles is where we pass beyond the grounds we may give 'for seeing the life and death of Jesus as a part of the human story which is of unique significance in relation to seeing the human story as a whole as a true story of divine redemption at work'.[9] The uniqueness of the gospel then seems to be exhausted in the special help we have to see divine redemption at work in the human story as a whole.

To sustain this view Professor Wiles has recourse to the notion of divine activity and the revelation of it as consisting essentially in some response of our own. A distinction seems to be implicit, in some of the ways Professor Wiles puts things, between the divine activity and responsiveness to it. But no serious account is taken of this, and all we have to go by is response—'it is in the experiencing of life as having the quality of response that the reality of divine action is known'.[10] It is in this way that 'God's action' is 'decisively revealed'[11] in certain events and not in others. Some people 'are more fully responsive to the divine action than others', and 'Their words and actions in turn will provide a particularly important focus for calling out such responses from others who follow them'.[12] In calling 'the events of their lives' 'special acts of God we would not be implying that there was any fundamental difference in the relation of the divine action to the particular worldly occurrences of their situation; we would be referring to the depth of response and the creative potential for eliciting further response from others embodied in those particular lives or those particular events'.[13] We are thus 'avoiding the error of thinking that we can ever describe divine action in any other context than that of its experienced response'.[14]

There is still some ambiguity. On the one hand we are told that we cannot 'speak significantly of God or of his acting in an objectified way, wholly separated from the human response',[15] and on the other of 'divine action' being 'most closely correlated with human responsiveness'.[16] Is there not, we must ask, anything above the human response?

On this Professor Wiles does not strictly commit himself, taking shelter instead in words like 'not wholly separated from' or 'closely correlated'. But the main impression we have is that nothing happens in redemptive activity and revelation over and above our own response and the way this may stimulate others to respond. There is certainly nothing to be laid upon or indicated besides the response any more than we can indicate some specific feature of events by which they are known to be created. For all the difference it makes, the responsiveness is all in all.

This is why we have 'to speak of an active God whose action is to be seen "in" rather than "between" worldly occurrences',[17] and it is not surprising therefore to see invoked again all the familiar paraphernalia of 'the logical oddity of religious language', 'experiencing as', and the new 'tools'.[18] The trouble is that 'response' may mean almost anything, we respond all the time to something or other. We respond to all sorts of persons and events, to Hitler as well as Gandhi, to ahimsa as to the holocaust, and there may be nothing specifically religious involved. Some ways of responding are indeed thoroughly reprehensible. Even when we hear of 'the depth of response' does this take us further? The positive response to Hitler was massive at one time, and if we wish to say that it was not deep, could we not speak of the deep or profound response of idealistic humanists who risked their lives to oppose him? In short, mere talk of response gets us nowhere—any more than attitude theories in ethics. We must hear more about the quality of the response, and is this likely to be meaningful without some account of what it is to which we respond? The weight which responsiveness as such is made to carry is out of all proportion.

The most that we are told, almost by accident, is that there is a 'response to an overall purpose at work in the world',[19] and that men have in this way 'found a meaning and a sense of purpose bigger than their own comparatively narrow concerns, being elicited as it were by the events of history'.[20] But here we are back at the beginning again—how do we discover this 'overall purpose' or acquire this 'meaning'? In our responsiveness to it? That would indeed be circular. Admittedly all forms of appreciation and insight require some kind of response, or, at the very least, attention. We have to respond to music and poetry to enjoy it but that is not the sole measure of the quality of the music or the poetry. In addition, there are secular as well as religious ways of claiming to find a purpose in history, the Marxist one usually giving a pre-eminent place to such purpose. What makes an overall purpose a religious one, what makes it Christian, and how do we come to discover it?

There have been many attempts, in the course of various philosophies of history and metaphysics, to clarify and justify the notion of a purpose in history. They all encounter formidable difficulties. Professor Wiles does nothing to alleviate these and sometimes gives the impression that he is not aware of them. But he does warn us not to seek confirmation of the alleged meaning of history either in some peculiarity of historical events or in *a priori* considerations or metaphysics, Anselm being called to task especially for taking the latter course in *Cur Deus Homo*. The divine activity is not 'in' but 'between' events. Quoting Professor Peter Baelz with approval, he assures us that the divine activity 'is fulfilled in the response which it evokes' and thus 'supernaturalises the natural';[21] and again there appears to be nothing for us to seize upon besides the response. Nor is it clear that even the response makes any difference to the course of things. The world would go on as it does anyway, or, as Bultmann had put it, 'the only thing generally visible and demonstrable is the "natural" occurrence', the rest being at most some sublime *epiphenomenon* if that—of the normal course of things, hidden to all but 'the eye of faith'.[22]

The role of Jesus, in this scheme of things, and such concessions as must be made to particularity, seems to be conceived in terms of 'the outstanding potency' of his life for eliciting 'the sense of response to purposive activity'.[23] Even Bultmann is rebuked for putting his own position in peril by his complementary stress on particularity. But suppose we ask further how does this 'outstanding potency' come about and how do we know about it? Christological belief, we are assured, at least 'includes a reference to the specific historical figure of Jesus'.[24] But how do we get at this figure? Have we any 'reliable knowledge of that life'?[25] Apparently not. The 'new quest' of the historical Jesus is no more successful than the old.[26] For, although we require to say, in some sense, that he is 'the embodiment of the divine', 'our knowledge about him in himself is at every point tentative and uncertain'.[27] We need not even consider whether we can 'ascribe an absolute authority to a particular section of experience within the world, such as the life of Jesus', for 'no such Jesus is available to us'.[28]

By contrast, 'We know Jesus, as we experience God, only in his effect upon the world, upon the church and upon ourselves'.[29] 'The information the theologian has traditionally looked for is simply not the kind of information that can properly be expected to be drawn from the evidence at our disposal by historical means'.[30] We have thus 'to acknowledge our inability to draw firm lines of demarcation between what is true of Jesus himself and what is true of the initial response to him revealed in the New Testament writings'.[31] There is a platitude in this which makes it difficult to comment. The New Testament writings were a response to Jesus, and it is in terms of this alone that we can know anything of substance about him. But this response includes memories and testimony. If no sort of reliability can be placed on that, one wonders just what is left of the response? One does not have to take everything at its face value in the New Testament. But that does not prevent us from forming a credible picture of what Jesus was like and what he did out of this material. The writers and those who prompted and inspired them were responding to someone whom they thought they knew in the terms they describe to us. If that has no validity, is there any significance in their response?

Professor Wiles, however, despairs, quite needlessly it seems to me, of getting at 'the true Jesus himself' in this or any other way. We must turn from his evidence as affecting simply Jesus himself to 'the whole event of his life and its impact on the world of the first century'[32] putting increased weight on 'the church's experience and understanding of Christ down the ages rather than historical reconstruction of his life and times'.[33] My own difficulty with the latter weighting is to know how it could matter without some core at least of initial dependable knowledge about Jesus. The experience of the saints can deepen our understanding of Christ but there must be something there to deepen.

I find it very difficult therefore to follow the 'move from concentration upon the individual figure of Jesus to the whole Christ event'.[34] How can there be a Christ event without a recognisable figure as the key to it? It is all very well to decry the notion that 'the epistles of St Paul embody divinely disclosed truths', coming presumably out of the blue of direct or literal inspiration, 'rather than one man's profound wrestling with the impact of Jesus on himself and his world'.[35] But how could this impact be made except on the basis of what St Paul had come to know about Jesus—and not only on the road to Damascus —and what we can sensibly accept on the evidence of the New Testament as a whole? St Paul was not wrestling with a shadow, and when we are told that we need not trouble much about the distinction between 'the contribution of Jesus himself and that of the evangelists',[36] we must reply that everything turns on how we set about making the distinction. If we seek to make it on formal considerations or independent evidence, we can hardly get off the ground; and that apparently is what has happened to so much New Testament study. Our scholars have got enmeshed in their own expertise. But we have no need to despair in this way if we try instead to listen to what sensitive, imaginative, perusal of the evidence tells us. We have all to demythologise in some measure and to make allowances for the beliefs and thought forms of the time. But it does not follow that everything must be dissolved into this, or that we do not have a very clear picture of the astonishing individual figure which made the impact on St Paul and others.

We may indeed know nothing about certain things apart from their effects. Invisible stars have been 'calculated' into existence in this way. But the effects must be distinctive to do this, and they tell us distinctive things about their causes, the size and exact location of the star for example. If the whole weight is to be put, in Christian belief, on the 'transforming impact'[37] or 'the transforming character of their experiences',[38] we need at least to be told a great deal about this transformation and patterns of response and the 'experience of redeeming grace in the lives of later Christians'[39] which make up the whole and continuing 'Christ event'. There are many transformations, some not so estimable as others. Is the test of truth here to be purely pragmatic? Have we nothing to go upon other than the lives of the saints or the changed character of Christian people and communities? If the change in question includes 'the practice of worship' and 'experience of redeeming grace', can we make much of this without the beliefs which inspired these things, and can we, without being hopelessly circular, simply test these against one another? Is the whole weight of the truth about Jesus to be made to rest on the quality of life of his followers, and how much weight can that bear? If we go beyond this and speak of deepening experience and 'redeeming grace', can we make this meaningful, in a Christian way, without certain beliefs about Jesus himself? Is the practice of worship sensible without those beliefs? In short, can we have a 'Christ event'—if the phrase is appropriate at all—without Christ?

Admittedly we cannot understand Jesus without much that we independently know about God and his ways. But this is a very different matter from claiming that confirmation of Christian experience 'must be looked for rather in reflection on what must be true to make sense of the religious understanding of the world as a whole to which the Christian tradition points'.[40] We have certainly moved very far from what would normally be understood by the divinity of Jesus when the weight is transferred in the way indicated to the 'Christ event' and responsiveness to the overall purpose of history. Can the same language and the same practices be retained in this new context? Should there not be more radical change of these as well? And what steps should we take to make sure that others are not misled?

Professor Wiles seems reluctant to drop the idea of incarnation altogether, and seems to think for this reason that we must retain some 'reference to the specific historical figure of Jesus'.[41] But the figure appears to be retained as a figurehead only to give some legitimacy, as it were, to the new establishment after the coup d'etat that toppled the traditional regime. Beyond that the traditional figure appears to be lost in the uncertainties of the 'Christ

event', and the latter in turn is drawn up into the vacuity
of its own responsiveness. It is too ethereal to be loved,
and too unreal to have its hands stretched on a cross. But
it was the victory of the real Christ who had been killed
that St Paul and other writers of the New Testament
proclaimed. It was this Christ, the Jesus who was in part
his own contemporary and of whom he had heard, from
the villages and around the shores of Galilee and in
Jerusalem, that was 'working' in him and 'exalted to the
right hand of God'. Is it not this Jesus who is also the
Christ for us today?

The idea of 'a Christ event' has however taken a very
deep hold, and it is attractive to many because it enables
us to set aside many of the most acute difficulties that
confront us in a more traditional view of the subject. One
redoubtable advocate of this new approach is Professor
Geoffrey Lampe, Ely Professor of Divinity at Cambridge.
He offers a sustained presentation of his view in his
Bampton Lectures, entitled *God as Spirit*.[42]
   The key to the theme of this book appears at the start in
the chapter 'Jesus is Alive Today'. We are told that
'Certainly, Paul believed that Christ was a contemporary,
personally existing being', but, it appears, this Christ,
'exalted to heaven' is also 'representative man'; 'The
Christ who is first-born from the dead is a corporate or
inclusive being, the head of the body, the church, and
moreover a cosmic being *in* whom all things in heaven
and on earth were created, *in* whom all things hold
together'.[43] 'He is a representative Christ, including or
summing up in himself all humanity'.[44] We read again:
'Paul's functional identification of "Christ" with Spirit in
many contexts, and his corporate and inclusive interpretation of Christ, suggest the possibility of using the
concept of the indwelling, life-giving, presence of God as
Spirit to articulate the real experience which underlines
the puzzling and misleading affirmation, "Jesus is alive
today"'.[45]
   Professor Lampe turns, in the same vein, to the Fourth
Gospel, where, it is claimed, Pentecost 'has certainly

become coincidental with Easter'.[46] 'To know Jesus Christ, here and now, is not to share the first disciples' experience of a personal presence, risen from the dead'.[47] For this reason 'believers can now, in some sense, transcend the Jesus of history'.[48] We have 'God himself as active towards and in his human creation';[49] 'through Jesus, God acted decisively to cause men to share in his relationship to God.'[50] 'Christ', we are told, 'is the focal point of the continuing encounter between God and man which takes place throughout human history'.[51] We are not, therefore, surprised to learn that human pride and selfishness bring upon men 'the suffering which God suffers, *incarnate* within them'.[52] 'God has always been incarnate in his human creatures, forming their spirits from within'.[53] This prepares for the central contention that 'the Christ whom we claim to be the central and focal point in the continuum of God's creative and saving activity is not only the historical Jesus; he is the complex of Jesus and his interpreters, a complex to which many minds have contributed, including that of the Fourth Evangelist'.[54]

The insistence that 'there is no other name' must be read in the 'proper context of Luke's reconstruction of the anti-Jewish apologetic of the primitive Church, and not generalised beyond that context'.[55] We do not need 'the concept of a post-existent continuing personal presence of Jesus, himself alive today, in order to interpret our own continuing experience of God's saving and creative work. The kingdom of God which Jesus called men to enter is here today. God the Spirit, who was present and acting in Jesus, is here today.'[56] And that, apparently, is all we need.

We come to the crux in the central chapter on 'Jesus and the Christ-event'. There is, we are told, 'a continuity of God's creative work in the process of cosmic evolution' but this came to a 'climax', 'a central and focal point', 'our key to the meaning of the process as a whole', the 'unbroken process' 'rising to a climax in Jesus Christ and proceeding through the subsequent course of human history with Jesus Christ as its reference point and determinant'.[57] 'Jesus stands within the succession of the prophets, differing from the rest in being "the" prophet who completes and perfects the work of all the others'.[58] Is this enough 'to support our Christian assertion of the decisiveness of Jesus Christ for the whole creative process'?[59] Professor Lampe thinks it is, when we also recall that 'a community did actually emerge in which men discovered the possibility of a new relationship to God', and where 'Conversion into sonship after the pattern of Jesus was an experienced reality'. [60]

Where precisely, in this setting, do we place the actual historical Jesus? On this Professor Lampe is not altogether explicit. He seems much attracted to the view—and certainly in no way perturbed by it—that 'the concrete individual person, Jesus of Nazareth, even if he became more directly accessible to historical investigation, could never carry this immense weight of theological significance'.[61] Christ, on the contrary, 'is an ideal or mythical person who symbolizes the goal to which that divine activity is tending'.[62] But this would be going too far. There is 'surely no need to abandon the historical Jesus as the actual source of the Christian experience of sonship and of the "fruit of the Spirit"'.[63] We must not exaggerate his 'strangeness' in allowing for 'the context of the society and culture of first-century Palestine',[64] for we 'have no reason to suppose that Jesus himself was quite unlike the person whom the Gospels depict'.[65] 'The Christ event, however, is a complex act of God', and 'the historical Jesus stands at the heart of it'.[66] Nevertheless, when we claim that Christ is 'the focal point which gives meaning to the whole, we are not speaking only of that historical figure and his words and deeds, but of a complex disclosure, focussed upon Jesus but not confined to him, of God's dealings with men'.[67]

This prompts many questions. I have never myself taken very kindly to the idea of 'corporate or inclusive being' or 'representative man'. This sort of hypostatisation has been the cause of many serious aberrations in philosophy and theological thinking at various times. It has often provided an escape route for those wishing to evade the demands of their commitment. My sins are not mine but those of some 'mass', the 'universal man' to which I belong, and I have stressed[68] how serious and far-reaching are the confusions which this imports into our understanding of sin and guilt, and how detrimental it is to a fair appreciation of moral responsibility and its place in religion. The unfortunate impact of it in social and political contexts was brilliantly displayed long ago by L. T. Hobhouse in his classic *The Metaphysical Theory of the State*,[69] and it would be a fine thing if this book were made compulsory reading for all theologians.

In the second place, the main reasons adduced by Professor Lampe for his scepticism regarding our knowledge of the historical Jesus seem to me very inadequate. No one need deny that Jesus was a man of his time and that much in the form of what he said and did belongs to a very different age from our own. But does this matter so much? It applies to all other great figures of antiquity, and indeed of periods much closer to our own. How sceptical do we need to be in making the appropriate allowances here? Are we to form no firm opinion about persons remote from our own times, and pass no judgment upon them? Is all history vain and hopelessly relative? The possibility of error, sometimes merely formal, in no way prevents us from coming to firm and highly plausible conclusions. We must not throw up our hands in despair because we have to use judgment and discernment and make reasonable allowance for an unfamiliar context. Consider how much has been very firmly established now, out of very meagre material, about Shakespeare.[70]

The argument which seems to weigh most with Professor Lampe, in the historical relativism to which he seems to succumb, is that 'we are unable to determine with complete certainty that the tradition behind any particular saying or story contained in these Gospels goes back to the historical Jesus himself' and 'a chain cannot be stronger than its individual links'.[71] This seems to overlook altogether the place of cumulative evidence, on which matters of the greatest moment are sometimes settled in our courts. If we detach each episode and look for some independent confirmation of it, we shall certaintly make no progress and must remain at best in a state of suspended judgment. But this is not how the portrait presents itself. We have to let imagination and sensitive insight play upon the evidence as a whole to sift what is substantial from what is incidental and peripheral. If theologians did not spend so much time sitting down to sharpen their tools, quite often the wrong ones, they would have got much further with their quest for the historical Jesus.

I cannot resist the temptation here to refer to a very remarkable inaugural lecture[72] delivered recently by my own successor in London, Professor Stewart Sutherland. He refers to the failure of Dostoyevsky, genius that he was, to achieve his long-entertained project of presenting a picture of perfect goodness, and the implication seems to be that the attempt is essentially misconceived, for perfect goodness cannot be netted in this way. It always eludes us when we set out in such fashion. But we can glimpse it if we know how to read the New Testament aright. We can give a new range to this witness, in word or deed; fine preaching achieves it, but with insight and not with a catalogue of virtues. The perils are evident in the many lives of Jesus, and in recent novels, even when attempted by well-informed and gifted writers. On the stage and in films the failures are shocking, and we wonder what advice, if any, lies behind them. Those who were close to the amazing reality caught it, their naivety itself being a help. If we also learn to look properly we can find the portrait convincing as historical fact and saving truth.

A further move which Professor Lampe makes with others of like mind today is again to present an unconvincing picture of the alternatives to his own view. He also tends to think that trinitarian doctrines, and variations on the attempts to cope with their problems, came directly, in the first instance, out of isolated scriptural contexts, and that thought of the divinity of Jesus took shape in this way. The reverse is the case. The trinitarian formulations are consequential and subsidiary, the divinity essential and direct. The disciples found they could respond in no other terms. Professor Lampe dwells much on the problems of how to conceive the pre-incarnation status of Jesus, on the assumption of his divinity, and even more his post-resurrection being. But do we have to do this? Is it not in the intricacies of byways of this kind that traditional theology lost the way? The incarnation is bound to remain a mystery, and is it not better to recognise where the veil falls, where we reach the limit of our comprehension of matters which the evidence none the less compels us to recognise?

One thing seems to me clear. It is as God—and nothing less—that orthodox Christians expect to meet Jesus in a future sanctified state, as in the present, and as he was encountered 'in the days of his flesh'. It is the same consciousness, with all its limitations as a human being by the lake in Galilee, that they also meet, and will meet. How this came about, by physical emergence from the tomb or in some other more mysterious way, is not vital. But Jesus in exaltation is the same consciousness as Jesus of Nazareth, and in both respects 'very God'. The tradition has never taken to the idea of three gods, but it has never wavered in the ascription of divinity to Jesus, however little this may have allowed of further comprehension. Nor, in my view, has it been affected as much as scholars today suppose by Gnostic and other ideas of a pre-existent logos. The central concern was with the essential mystery of God made man, and if, understandably and regrettably, they went further than they should in seeking to set out explicitly the ramifications of a triune God, the stance which initially prompted this was a sound and unavoidable one. That is where they began, and when they looked forward to sanctified fellowship with Christ, they were thinking of him as the same consciousness as Jesus in Nazareth and Jerusalem, being also God, and not in any way as the continuation of the divine activity in the hearts and minds of men generally.

This, whatever its problems, is where the tradition stands, and, if we cannot take it, then, I submit, we need far more drastic changes in ritual practice and declaration

of faith to come into better accord with the more attenuated claims now being made. The earlier unitarians took
the force of this, with clarity and integrity. There is a limit
to the adaptations that are possible. For my own part I feel
no obligation to make them, for what is essential in
traditional form and practice stands unimpaired, indeed
more clearly in much that we shed, in a faith that centres
on the uniqueness of the individual Jesus rather than the
ambiguities of a 'Christ event'.

It does not follow that there may not be a great
deepening of understanding and appreciation, of finer
praise and profounder worship, as we draw into our own
experience the experience of others, today and in the past.
In this sense a faith can be dynamic and corporate, and it
will continue to evolve, but always on 'the Church's one
foundation', 'Jesus Christ the Lord'.

The third example to which I wish to refer is a very
intriguing and significant one, but also peculiarly difficult
to handle. This is because the writer in question, while
presenting, in essentials, the same sort of theme as that of
Professor Lampe, is even more determined to bring it into
line with traditional attitudes and confessions of faith,
especially in the shape they took at Chalcedon and to
claim their sanction or at least their support. He is
Professor James P. Mackey, recently appointed to the
Chair of Christian Dogmatics at Edinburgh, and author of
another much-publicised book[73] described in the blurb as
'perhaps unequalled, for all the recent competition, since
Schweitzer's famous Quest'.

There is much that can be conceded to Professor
Mackey's views, and much that is very effectively put. But
here again, when we feel that we are closing in on our
quarry, everything seems to melt away into uncertainty.
Consider briefly first his view of the resurrection of Jesus.
It is firmly admitted that 'the myth known as the resurrection' 'contained within itself as an essential part of it
the belief that the individual Jesus himself lives beyond his
death, that Jesus of Nazareth lives with God, that the

tomb did not see the end of that particular person'.[74] But this can not be taken just by itself. The mere 'revival of a corpse' would prove very little, and we are reminded that St Paul, as a devout Pharisee, 'did not need witnesses to a proof-miracle to prove that the dead would be raised . . . for he was already in possession of such belief'.[75] There is no need to dispute any of this, and I do not think anything vitally turns on whether the individual Jesus is alive, in spite of death, because he emerged from the tomb or in some other way, provided we are clear that it was 'the individual Jesus', 'that particular person'. Attempts to make everything rest on an empty tomb seem to me very misguided. The resurrection is not some one pivot apart; other persons are said to have come back to life without any further special claim being made for them. The resurrection must be taken in relation to everything else we are told about Jesus.

On the other hand we move into somewhat uncertain terrain when we read that 'the New Testament writers on resurrection are not so much interested in the fact that Jesus lived again by God's act after he had died' as in 'a new dynamic role which he plays in what they believe to be the divine direction of our history in this universe'.[76] Does this mean that the belief that Jesus lived again has a very subsidiary place and may even be dispensed with in relation to the 'role he plays'? It is hard to avoid that conclusion when we also read, in the same passage, that 'the myths which move at the depth of human experience . . . do not convey any literal information about worlds other than this one or about beings other than those we meet in this empirical world of ours'. 'Literal' is a difficult word here. We can only speak with great caution about what another world or existence may be like, but does this mean that we must stay at the level of a 'promise for the continuity and increase of life' and 'life-enhancing elements'?[77] Jesus came, as we all know, that we may 'have life more abundantly', but this is usually under-stood in relation to a very special fellowship with him. How much of that is retained in these 'life-enhancing elements'? Very little, one is inclined to suspect, in the

down-grading of the belief in the continued existence of
Jesus.

The prophets present us with 'life-enhancing elements';
so did Gandhi and so did many a fine secularist like Gilbert
Murray. Was Jesus just doing the same in a superlative
degree? Is this the substance of 'the resurrection'?

Let us look more closely at the 'dynamic role' ascribed
to Jesus. We understand this on the basis of the central
idea, for Professor Mackey, of 'the faith of Jesus'. All
really hinges on this. This faith is 'the lived experience/
evaluation/acceptance of all life and existence as gift or
grace',[78] to see 'all things great and small as the gift or
grace of God to all';[79] 'It is a living attitude to all things
and especially to all people, a life-gesture of receiving as
gift, rather than grasping and tearing loose', and this
involves also 'a distinctive lived conviction of the immediacy of God in the very contingency of our existence'.[80]
It is not 'primarily a set of moral precepts or ritual acts' but
'a life lived'.[81] This is 'the faith of Jesus' and people 'are
brought into contact with the living God' because Jesus
inspired them to such faith.[82]

This is finely put, but is it enough? Professor Mackey
certainly thinks so. He tells us that 'the faith of Jesus' is
also 'the faith of others' because of 'Jesus's life inspiring
and infecting them' and thus 'To say that they encounter
the one, true God in the faith of Jesus is to say what that
faith is, to say simultaneously that it was the very life of
the man Jesus, and that it is theirs because it was his; and
all this can be abbreviated in the formula that they meet in
Jesus the one, true God'.[83]

It is at this point that Professor Mackey parts company
with Bultmann, to whom he is peculiarly indebted. For
Bultmann 'the object of our Christian faith is the Christ of
the proclamation, the risen Lord rather than the historical
Jesus',[84] though this was not based mainly on distrust of
the historical sources. But Professor Mackey will not have
this 'dichotomy between faith and history'. The actual,
individual Jesus matters, and he matters essentially,
because it is in the 'faith of Jesus', in his lived life, that we
have made available to us, inspired by him, the same

conviction of the immediacy of God in the contingency of existence and the givenness of all things. This faith of Jesus 'alone provides our encounter with the one, true God, whom we cannot directly "see" or "hear"; a conviction that the historic person of Jesus, himself a man of such faith, is for us the source of this faith, the one person in our history who inspires and empowers us to such faith; the one, therefore, in whom we encounter the one, true God'.[85]

In this vein Professor Mackey sets out to defend Chalcedon—himself a knight of orthodoxy. We must, he maintains, against both Arius and Apollinarius, preserve the full humanity of Jesus which they had put in peril. The 'human soul of Jesus' is not to be 'entirely replaced by the divine Logos or Word';[86] nor was it the case that the soul-less body of a man was inhabited by some divine intermediary, 'a lesser divinity', 'at once too small to be equal to the One, and too large to be circumscribed in human terms'.[87] The full humanity of Jesus, 'the man of flesh, the man of faith',[88] must be preserved; at the same time, what we encounter in Jesus is 'not a lesser divinity, but Very God'.[89]

This seems fine. What more could an orthodox traditional Christian require? The claims of Chalcedon seem to be fully endorsed. But are they in fact, or only formally? Christ is fully man, and in him we also encounter 'Very God'. But 'encounter' is a deceptive word. To encounter God in Jesus is one thing, even when it is a supreme encounter; to find him to *be* God is another. It sounds fine to say that, as 'the faith of Jesus is the life of a man', 'Jesus is not simply an enlightener, prophet, or bearer of formulated divine truth, but the human person in whom God fully and truly encounters humanity in history'.[90] But some of this could also be said of many prophets: they are not just bearers of 'formulated divine truth', they have a 'lived life'. Is the difference just one of degree? More directly, does the notion of being inspired and empowered by Jesus to share his own faith get us anywhere near the meaning that would normally be accorded to the phrase 'the divinity of Jesus'?

One suspects that Professor Mackey is not giving us all that he seems to give when he writes 'that in Jesus' human existence we encounter God, and yet we encounter only Jesus'.[91] This is again very difficult to handle. For it is quite true that we encounter 'only Jesus', in his full humanity. But 'only Jesus' is also, not in some peculiar respects, but through and through, in all that he is as a human being, divine. His divinity is not some quality of the human faith he has, nor some special way in which he communicates this. It is what he is himself in his whole person. If we cannot take that, if the humanity is thereby imperilled, would it not be better to say so bluntly rather than seek further subtle ways in which the same set of terms may be used, far removed from the initial intention when we look closely at what is being offered?

Professor Mackey, like Professor Lampe, makes a great deal also of the idea of 'Spirit'—'the spirit of Jesus, by which his very person is identified, shaped and still shapes the world of our common experience';[92] and we have also a peculiar use of 'transcendence'. We have the very questionable view of divinity as 'both transcendent and immanent', for how could God be both except in the sense which alone is seriously intended of being 'effective' in the world. There is a similar rash use of 'emanation'. It is puzzling also to read of 'human transcendence' present 'in any area of human creativity'.[93] Are we not on a slippery slope here also?

The crux in all these matters (and after all I have said very similar things to Professor Mackey and find my heart warming to much that he says) comes about when we consider just what motivates him to offer an attenuated view, as it seems to me, of the proper divinity of Jesus. He is very anxious—and are we not all?—to continue 'to conceive of Jesus as one single individual'.[94] To speak of 'two natures', even more 'two intellects' etc., comes perilously close to dividing the one individual. We must not, he very properly warns us, think 'crudely of the divinity of Jesus', much less suppose that it is 'some "person" or "thing" lodged within the man, Jesus'.[95] For even if we only veer in this direction we put ourselves at once in danger that we 'make virtually impossible any intelligible statement of the unity of Jesus' person'.[96] This, I feel sure, is what mainly motivates Mackey and the other scholars I have discussed. If we take the incarnation seriously, and in the most full-blooded sense, how can we possibly make sense of it? If we take 'Very God' to mean what it says, must we not somehow impair or limit the proper humanity of Jesus? And that, it is very rightly stressed, is to fall headlong into the worst pitfall for today. However much we speak of being 'undivided' and 'unconfused', can we make sense of this without some diminishing of what we mean?

If we give up on the attempt to make sense of the seeming contradiction of God in fully human form, 'it is all', it would seem, 'assertion and no explanation'.[97] It is sheer dogmatism which we are tempted to relieve by drifting once more 'towards the attractive sirens of Apollinarius'.[98] But is it as fatal as all that, is it a vicious dogmatism, to say that we just cannot understand how God could so limit himself that, being always and essentially God, he would also undergo fully the 'lived life' of a man? A transcendent being is always in essentials beyond our comprehension; an element of mystery and bewilderment affects all our thinking at this level. We must not exploit this to justify irrational and irresponsible thinking in theology or philosophy, though I fear that this has in fact often happened. All the same it is only in mediated ways, through our own experience and history, that we come to know God; and if the evidence, in our sensitive appreciation of the figure who comes to us out of the available New Testament records, leaves us at the point where we can only say, reverently, but firmly, this must be God himself, not just truth about him, in this 'lived life', this individual consciousness, should we draw back, can we honestly do so, because we have no understanding of how this could possibly be? It is no blind dogmatism, no desperate clinging to tradition, to recognise in humility what is forced upon us when we cannot explain it further but simply declare that this is how it seems to be.

This extends also, as surely it must if it holds at all, to the way we continue to think of Jesus in his abiding oneness with God. There is no division, no two persons. When the saints speak of meeting Jesus, in a further transformed and sanctified state, they expect to meet him as he was encountered, whether men realised it or not, in the days of his flesh as God. And when we meet God we meet Jesus, the individual consciousness that people met in Galilee or Jerusalem. The incarnation was once for all, for a little over thirty years, but Jesus is for all time and eternity.

These are themes I have presented more fully elsewhere. I must leave them as they stand for the present. But in the meantime I must declare, if I may end on a personal note in this lecture, that when we encounter what seem to me increasingly implausible substitutes for what, in common sense, we would take to be the central and lasting themes of the New Testament, and of Christian experience and witness throughout the ages, when not only all miracle—and do we have to abandon miracle altogether?—but all reasonably reliable knowledge and understanding of the historical Jesus, all firm expectation of 'life beyond' and a sanctified condition of ourselves in fellowship with God through the mediation of Jesus, however unlikely in our normal understanding of ourselves, when this and all thought of God as abidingly one with the individual Jesus we meet in the story is lost in the mists of ambiguous secular expectations—then, I can only say, in the words of a desolate woman of long ago, 'they have taken away my lord and I know not where they have laid him'. It is comforting to think that it was in the depth of this despair that she was personally addressed and assurance flooded in, overwhelming. May we not also, in the blackness of so much despair, hear the same voice addressing us by name today?

NOTES

1. Maurice Wiles, 'Does Christology Rest on a Mistake?', *Religious Studies*, vol. 6 (1970) pp. 69–76. Cf. his 'Religious Authority and Divine Action', *Religious Studies*, vol. 7 (1971) pp. 1–12.
2. 'Does Christology rest on a mistake?', p. 71.
3. Ibid., p. 72.
4. Ibid., p. 72.
5. Ibid., p. 74.
6. Ibid., p. 74.
7. Ibid., p. 75.
8. Hywel D. Lewis, 'Ultimates and a Way of Looking' in *Persons and Life After Death* (London: Macmillan, 1978).
9. 'Does Christology Rest on a Mistake?', p. 75.
10. 'Religious Authority and Divine Action', op. cit., p. 6.
11. Ibid., p. 7.
12. Ibid., p. 7.
13. Ibid., p. 7.
14. Ibid., p. 7.
15. Ibid., p. 9.
16. Ibid., p. 9.
17. Ibid., p. 4.
18. I have never taken very kindly to the familiar talk, by philosophers as well as theologians, of 'tools'. It seems to me to suggest a very wrong way of going about things, but the avidity, and pride, with which theologians speak in this way is amazing, and I hope it is not too flippant, in the context of such very serious issues as the present one, to recall an occasion when I nearly managed to persuade one chairman of the Board of Studies in Theology in London, when we were considering what applications might be made from the faculty grant for equipment, to order for us a couple of Occam's razors, hinting that there might be one or two good second-hand ones lying around at Oxford. Unhappily Principal Copleston was present and, his mirth bursting all bounds, exploded and cast doubt on the seriousness of my intentions.
19. Ibid., p. 5.
20. Ibid., p. 5.
21. Ibid., p. 8.
22. Ibid., p. 3.
23. 'Religious Authority and Divine Action', p. 6.
24. Maurice Wiles, *The Remaking of Christian Doctrine* (London: SCM Press, 1974) p. 45.
25. Ibid., p. 47.
26. 'The 'new quest' of the historical Jesus may have overcome some of the particular problems of the 'old quest'; it has not escaped its fundamental difficulty. Nor is any subsequent quest likely to do so.' Ibid., p. 47.
27. Ibid., p. 49.

28. Ibid., p. 48.
29. Ibid., p. 49.
30. Ibid., p. 48.
31. Ibid., p. 50.
32. Ibid., p. 50.
33. Ibid., p. 50.
34. Ibid., p. 50.
35. Ibid., p. 51.
36. Ibid., p. 52.
37. Ibid., p. 52.
38. Ibid., p. 53.
39. Ibid., p. 55.
40. Ibid., p. 59.
41. Ibid., p. 45.
42. G. Lampe, *God as Spirit* (Oxford: Clarendon Press, 1977).
43. Ibid., p. 4.
44. Ibid., p. 5.
45. Ibid., p. 6.
46. Ibid., p. 9.
47. Ibid., p. 8.
48. Ibid., p. 10.
49. Ibid., p. 11.
50. Ibid., p. 11.
51. Ibid., p. 13.
52. Ibid., p. 22 (my italics).
53. Ibid., p. 23.
54. Ibid., p. 27.
55. Ibid., p. 31.
56. Ibid., p. 33.
57. Ibid., p. 96.
58. Ibid., p. 97.
59. Ibid., p. 97.
60. Ibid., p. 97.
61. Ibid., p. 103.
62. Ibid., p. 103.
63. Ibid., p. 103.
64. Ibid., p. 103.
65. Ibid., p. 102.
66. Ibid., p. 104.
67. Ibid., p. 104.
68. Hywel D. Lewis, *Morals and the New Theology*, Chapters v–ix (London: Victor Gollancz, 1947).
69. L. T. Hobhouse, *The Metaphysical Theory of the State* (London: Allen & Unwin, 1918).
70. M. C. Bradbrook, *Shakespeare, the Poet and his World* (New York: Columbia University Press, 1978) and related writing.
71. G. Lampe, op. cit., p. 102.

72. Stewart Sutherland, *Goodness and Particularity* (1979). Printed privately and obtainable from King's College, The Strand, London.
73. James P. Mackey, *Jesus, the Man and the Myth* (London: SCM Press, 1979).
74. Ibid., p. 194.
75. Ibid., p. 96.
76. Ibid., p. 194.
77. Ibid., p. 195.
78. Ibid., p. 162.
79. Ibid., p. 231.
80. Ibid., p. 231.
81. Ibid., p. 231.
82. Ibid., p. 230.
83. Ibid., p. 231.
84. Ibid., p. 252.
85. Ibid., p. 238.
86. Ibid., p. 242.
87. Ibid., p. 234.
88. Ibid., p. 233.
89. Ibid., p. 233.
90. Ibid., p. 232.
91. Ibid., p. 247.
92. Ibid., p. 260.
93. Ibid., p. 261.
94. Ibid., p. 244.
95. Ibid., p. 241.
96. Ibid., p. 241.
97. Ibid., p. 244.
98. Ibid., p. 245.

Appendix A: Christology Today

An extract from a Presidential Address delivered to the Oxford Society for the Study of Theology, and published in part as below in *The Modern Free Churchman* No. 97 Spring 1973.

Whatever death means for us, it meant for Jesus. But how then can we speak of this limited distinct being, moving around in the circumscribed way of the rest of us, in many respects the creature of his time, undoubtedly limited in knowledge and understanding—how can we speak of him as God except in some extremely diluted sense, as in idealist or pantheist philosophies or as a wholly metaphorical way of saying that we see more of God in him than in any other or that it is in knowing him that we come to know God best? How can we go beyond this and affirm a genuine identity when such identification of persons is in any case precluded[1] and above all when we remind ourselves that the idea of God is the idea of a being who is not only superior in power and goodness to ourselves but also eternal, uncreated, absolute in power and goodness in some way that is altogether beyond our comprehension? Are not the Greek and the Jew and the Muslim dead right here? Are we not as Christians persisting in commending something, out of some inveterate holding to a confused tradition, which no man in his senses can begin to consider today? A man just could not be God.

Or if he could how could he? I have stressed the difficulty, partly to show that I understand well the attractiveness of attenuated notions of incarnation such as are common today. I will only add on that score what I have said already about the misleading character of a half-hearted and obscure affirmation of a notion we cannot really accept. Let us stop talking in terms of incarnation if we find that we cannot take it. Let us ask what can be salvaged for Christianity without it and let us be honest with ourselves and others about this. Do not let us pretend that we are holding on to the substance if we have to give it up.

But do we have to give it up? I do not for a moment think so. And I say this, not in the sense that we could not have any proper form of Christianity without it, but because it seems to me just overwhelmingly true. It is this unbelievable thing that we have to proclaim, and one factor in our failure to proclaim it with success and take proper advantage of the tremendous renewal of interest in religion, is that we just do not believe it ourselves. But then how can we believe something that is so completely incomprehensible to us?

It is just here that it is so very tempting to look for ways of making the central Christian affirmation at least a little more comprehensible. Perhaps we can find a new philosophical model or a new analogy extracted from some feature of our life today or of new ways of understanding the world around us. I myself however hold out no hope of this kind. New metaphors may help where others are getting too familiar or stale. But they can offer no way of reducing the radically paradoxical nature of the affirmation that a man was also God.

But in that case what are we doing? Are we not just doing what I have accused Barth and his followers of doing? We are digging our heels in and saying, 'Well, this is the faith, we do not propose to give it up; if we are thereby committed to unreason, that cannot be helped, so much the worse for reason'. I certainly do not recognise myself in this description and I have not the slightest inclination to keep company with impossible exploiters of unreason. But I realise that I do come formally very close to them, or may seem to do so at this point.

For if I am pressed to say how we can possibly make
any sense of the Christian idea of incarnation I must reply
at once that I cannot, and that it is the great mistake of
many theologians today to try. On the other hand I must
hasten to insist that I do not believe blindly, at this point
or any other. I do not will or decide to believe, and I do
not believe without adequate grounds. My understanding
is very much involved in my apprehension of these
grounds. What are they? They are what we find in the
Gospels and the New Testament generally. This must not
be understood mechanically. We have all been told over
and over that the Gospels are not biographies or immediate recordings, like most of the Qur'an. We must use
historical sense and common sense. But just how could
these records have come about without an individual who
lived and taught substantially what they present? There
are some passages, surprisingly few and relatively trivial,
which cannot be easily harmonised with the rest, like the
passage about the two swords or cursing the fig tree. But
it is not all that hard to see how these could be distortions
of something that takes its place properly in the picture.
The surprising thing is how marvellously consistent the
picture is in essentials, even when it is also most un-
expected. It does not worry me much, indeed not at all,
that scholars can find anticipations or prototypes of much
that is ascribed to Jesus as part of his teaching in other
places. We all can in a measure—and we need not go
further than remarkable passages of the Old Testament to
do so. But where does one begin to find such an extraordinary range and wealth of insight, altogether un-
expected but unerringly right when it comes, absolute
and irresistible but not impersonal, clothed in the simplest
forms within the reach of all and alive and real to all. It is
not a formal system, and that is perhaps what is meant in
the extraordinary claim that some have made that there is
no ethics in the New Testament. The peculiar sort of
selflessness that is reflected in the whole body of the New
Testament, even when it tends to harden into doctrinaire
harshness, the unaffected character of it, the dignity
without pretentiousness, the absolutely right variations in

all the varieties of the forms in which it appears, with young and old, with happy people, with distressed people, with sophisticated men and with simple-minded, with professional people, with crowds, with close associates, sometimes very understanding and sometimes naïve, with various forms of hostility, some vicious, some stupid. Where in all this, and in much besides which we do not properly present at all in a bald summary but only in the actual astonishing records, where in all this do we begin to find anything that has a parallel before or after?

But it is not just a remarkable body of insight into what men should do and how they should live together that we have. Even that is without a peer, but here we have it as something lived out in a way of which the records contain no hint of imperfection or departure. Admittedly the witnesses are not altogether impartial, they are stating their case, as has often been stressed. But we should not be daunted too much by this. There is a sharp limit to what they could have doctored in this kind of material, and it is much too remarkable and out of line with normal expectations for us to suppose that it was concocted, especially by a number of different authors. The writers were working on the basis of material already available and shaped very close indeed to the events in question; and while it is well known that legends of all kinds grow up very quickly around impressive and notable people, and that there is little limit to popular credulity, it still remains impossible to suppose that the substance of what is presented about the teaching and the life of Jesus is not the truth; and if there had been some disconcerting or embarrassing factor to be reckoned with also, there would surely have been at least an oblique indication of it in the record. There is none, and the quality of what we have makes it further improbable in the extreme that there could be any.[2]

All these are matters which many Biblical experts can put much better than I, although I think the philosopher is entitled to warn the Biblical expert against certain preconceptions to which he is prone, including a caution which is apt to degenerate into cultivated scepticism and an occasionally narrow notion of how the main facts could be established. I shall return to that. But let me quote just two sentences from a splendid passage in Mr. John Baker's book, *The Foolishness of God*.

'There is the shrewd sense of humour, the reverence for children, the gift of poetry, the devastating anger; and yet the rejection of the solutions imposed by force. We then begin to feel we "know" him, in the way we might know a great figure of our own times whom we have heard and seen on television or in the papers, perhaps in the flesh, or whose biography we have read'.

Let me return then to my point about the evidence. The important thing is the impression of Jesus which emerges for us from the New Testament as the relevant material is sifted by judicious understanding. But it must be added that it is not merely the ethical teaching of Jesus that matters here and his own remarkable loyalty to it, though that is certainly central. There is also his sense of spiritual reality, of the presence of God and of the way our various situations are invested with a spiritual or transcendent significance; in other words the insight is as remarkable at this level, and in the extraordinary balance of the more secular and the more sacred elements in our total ex-perience. Of his own sense of his peculiar nearness to God and of a distinctive rôle he had to play in con-sequence of this, I shall say nothing at this point.[3] For I believe that our final assessment of that depends on our response to the material that is otherwise evident to us, as I hope to stress again in due place.

But what do we do with the evidence, as I have here called it? We certainly do not draw a series of formal deductions from it. It is more like the evidence which builds itself up into our impression of the magnificence of a great work of art. Reason is involved in this, and creatures of low mentality could not attain it, there is a discipline; but it is not strictly parallel to formal deduction or the confirmation of a scientific hypothesis. A very special insight is involved all along; and thus if one declares *Hamlet* to be a great masterpiece, there is a great deal one can explicitly say in support of this, and literary critics and laymen alike will go on saying it. But none of that is possible without the proper appreciation at all points of the excellence of what is unfolded for us, both in the use of words and in the delineation of various characters and their situation. I do not want to labour unduly the analogy with the arts, and I agree, as I have also stressed elsewhere, that it needs to be handled very carefully. But what I have especially in mind at the moment is the build-up of an overall impression in which it is not easy, or perhaps possible, to single out precisely the contribution of the various elements on their own.

It is thus, I think, that we 'see Jesus'. We live with the evidence, helped by all the illumination available to us from those who have trod this way before; we take it into the very substance of our own life, we create it anew with sanctified imagination, we leave it and come back to it, we take heed of our own suggestibility and the thoughts that come naturally from our background, and we have to ask ourselves what it amounts to. Even Buber, not himself a Christian, found it impossible to classify Jesus. But it is not just a question of classification. It all goes beyond that, the situation gets almost out of hand. For we must on the one hand view the circumstances against the background of all that we find, in the ways outlined earlier, that God had been working already in the world and in history — and this I take to be indispensable. But we also find that the culmination which the process has in the coming of Jesus breaks the bounds of that very process itself. This is not another prophet, not even a supreme one, not just another magnificent martyr. The blend of all that is so unexpectedly appropriate in this one person, against circumstances some of which were favourable, and some very unfavourable in his day, confronts us with a reality of which no normal account is possible. It is so full of God, as already known in part 'in sundry times and in diverse manners', that it could only be explicitly God himself. It is too completely of God to be secondary. There is no doubt mediation and a tempering to what we can stand. But that concerns the form, not the substance here. We are not indeed—how could we be?—face to face with the Godhead, but it is, on the other hand, not a case of God just making himself known to us through ourselves or other men, it is a person who is himself God. Only God himself could be this, and that is itself something we can only see to be inevitable in the presence of the evidence as it becomes properly alive to us. The injunction in the Gospels is 'come and see'. This is all we can do, but I submit that what we do see is a person between whom and the being of God there is no division. They are completely one, not in purpose or accordance of will but in reality.

And yet Jesus lived a temporal life with all the limitations fully conceded already. He was not a phantom but a man. What of our paradox? This is where I may seem to some of you to run away, as I have often accused others of doing. I must just say that I do not know the answer. That it must somehow be possible with God seems to me clear, and while it is certainly a fair demand to ask me why I am driven to this strange conclusion, I must exert myself along the lines indicated already to show just how this sort of conviction arises and what materials are relevant to it and how. But beyond this there is nothing one can do, and *we defeat ourselves if we try*. On the other hand it is not improper to insist that what defeats all comprehension by us is not impossible for God. The contradiction in which we seem to be involved is not some tangle within our finite understanding of finite things. I am not, like Niebuhr if my understanding of him is fair, invoking the transcendent to justify sticking with contradictions in our explanation of ethical or some other secular situation as such. I simply hold that while, in any normal context, what I affirm would not be tolerable at all, in the case of God it must *somehow* be possible for Him, without ceasing to be God (which is not possible anyhow) to live out the temporal span of a human life as we also live it and die as we die. We are sometimes asked, 'But do you think that God has Jesus's experiences?' I think we must answer, with all humility, 'Yes', or at least that 'Yes' is the least misleading answer we can give. Of course in one sense

God has everyone's experiences. He knows us as we know ourselves, although without depriving us of the freedom to be ourselves and sometimes go against his will. But this is one thing, and we must not prevaricate. I mean, in my own affirmation, more than this, more than that God is in one sense all in all. He had the experiences of Jesus as Jesus, in fully human form, had them and yet without ceasing to be God, infinite in wisdom and majesty. It was somehow possible for this to be, God being God, though *how* it is altogether impossible for us to know, as impossible in principle as anything can be.

At this point the critic, especially today with the verification doctrine still not very far behind us, will rear himself up in very firm protest: 'But how can you affirm anything which is totally incomprehensible to you? This is equivalent to affirming nothing at all. You just cannot know what you are saying'. I reply that in one essential sense I do know. I know how we come to know that there is God and how he discloses himself in human experience and I claim, on the basis of what is presented about Jesus against this background that there must be an absolute identity of the being of Jesus and God. All this bristles with difficulties, with which the apologist claims he can cope. He is not saying something further out of the blue, he can indicate how he is compelled to say it, and he is not precluded from doing that, under the impression of the appropriate evidence, by the fact that he is also at this point beyond the possibility of further explication. There is obviously a severe limit to all talk about God; if you allow it at all you must allow it in those terms; and it is this that makes exploitation easy. The apologist has to be on his guard not to make things, for that reason, too easy for himself or seeming to do so. But I myself find that, while the facts compel me to affirm, in the way indicated, the identity of God and Jesus, this is the point where further understanding is not possible. We just see what must be the case. We see this without seeing in the slightest measure *how* it can be. On the 'how' the veil falls totally for us. This is what has been overlooked in much subtle theology in the past; it is seriously overlooked today, as in doctrines of continuous incarnation or of explanatory models taken from fashionable philosophy.

NOTES

1. See Hywel D. Lewis, *The Elusive Mind* (London: Allen & Unwin, 1969) where I offer a sustained defence of the finality of the distinctness of persons.
2. This is where I find the position of Bonhoeffer in his *Christology*, even allowing that it is an immature work, exceptionally hard to understand. He defends in a very absolute way 'the incognito of the incarnation'. In pursuance of this he is quite happy to say that 'One can and should see good and bad' in the deeds of Jesus. One wonders what are the bad things? If one has to recognise them, then all is not lost. We can learn from Jesus as from other notable but fallible and erring men, we can still admire and follow him in the main respects—we cannot worship him. Remarks like those of Bonhoeffer, coming not from a hostile source but from an apologist, are the sort which send a shudder down one's back. Is it not time we began to realise that heroism is no guarantee of soundness of judgement—or even common sense?
3. But I would like to draw attention to a scholarly discussion of this question by H. P. Owen 'The New Testament and the Incarnation: A Study in Doctrinal Development', *Religious Studies*, vol. 8, Number 3, September (1972).

Appendix B: Fiction and Spiritual Debility

(Reproduced with permission from an article in *The Times* 14 June 1969.)

In appraising the plays of Shakespeare, our reason is heavily involved but it does not offer formal or scientific proof of what we think of them. Something similar is also true of religion, especially in dealing with figurative terms.

Once these are wrested out of context and the live experiences which they reflect, they become treacherous. They have led, for instance, to very unchristian ideas of an angry God invoking the full rigour of the law or of paying ransom to the devil. It is in the context of a personal relationship that we understand how we are 'bought' and the price that was paid. Nor does this become trivial. We can truly say that 'the Son of Man is come to seek and to save that which is lost'. But we must understand this in its true and most profound sense.

To do so we need to clear away confusions due to a failure to distinguish between the religious strands and the ethical ones in notable situations in which they have been much conflated. A sense of our littleness before God is not the same as moral guilt or its deepened sense in religion. Above all we must grasp how our own wrong-doing affects our inner life. Here, of course, we must first realize that we have a life within. The denial of this has been one of the greatest and most unfortunate mistakes made by recent philosophy in English-speaking countries.

There is what Bertrand Russell has so vividly described (in Vol. II of his *Autobiography*, p. 157) as 'the sense of sombre solitude', closely associated with 'the fear that enters the soul through experience of the major evils to which life is subject'. This is a side of our finite nature with which we must come to terms, above all in religion. The sense of deliberate wrong upsets the balance and drives us in on ourselves; then the inwardness becomes dominant, even when the outward round of our lives remains normal. We succumb to a sense of unreality or spiritual debility, that failure of involvement so strikingly portrayed in a remarkable recent novel by John O'Hara, *The Instrument.*

Indeed, what recent philosophers have rather brashly denied seems peculiarly evident in art and fiction and films. With great insight and delicate execution recent novelists from Edmund Wilson to Iris Murdoch have portrayed the situation that religion is about. We are, moreover, the heirs of much that has gone wrong in these ways in the past: and ourselves deepen the 'sombre solitude' of others, which is a very different thing from being to blame for one another.

Some religions cope with this by acceptance, by heightening the sense of unreality and looking to the ultimate dissolution of oneself and the world. Christianity is a realistic religion. It deepens the sense of personal existence and also heals and reclaims us in the coming of God, forsaken and destroyed, into the heart of our own lostness. There can be no adequate relation of ourselves to our world, our fellows or to God, except in confrontation with this—now or hereafter. This is the sole universal salve, without which the cancer of an inner unreality brings on pangs of despair and dissolution—and of deep and relentless remorse.

'Whip me, ye devils—Wash me in steepdown gulfs of liquid fire'. Words from the Bible? Or an evangelistic sermon? Not a bit. They are a quotation from *Othello,* reproduced in a daring novel whose publication was the cause of a celebrated court case (*The Philanderer* by Stanley Kauffman).

I do not suggest that we can infer the whole substance of Biblical teaching from contemporary fiction. Far from it—that would be the attenuation against which we must guard closely. But these writers tell us a great deal that sets us on the way, and do so more effectively and to a better audience than we do in the pulpit. That is one of the most helpful signs of our times.

4 Christ and Other Faiths

There have been two main themes in what I have maintained in my earlier lectures. The first is that we cannot make real sense of Christianity and its practice, or do any justice to the New Testament, without a genuine historical Jesus, not in the limited sense which Professor Lampe seemed disposed to allow, namely that there must have been a historical person behind the legends and the rise of Christianity, but in the much more vital and essential sense that we have a distinct unmistakable picture of this person as the basis of the special claims which the Christian faith has, with justification in essentials in my view, made about him. We know what he was like, and this is all-important.

This does not mean, and I doubt whether it has ever been very seriously thought to mean, that everything in the gospels, even the synoptic gospels, must be taken at its face value, as literal truth. A great deal at least in the nativity stories is legend and peripheral to the essential claims of the Gospel. No intelligent and informed person supposes today that the miracles all happened in the order in which they are described. They do not come in the same order in the different gospels, and versions of them vary. Some wear the look of parables more than of miraculous events. Opinions will vary on the importance to be attached to them. I believe that some certainly happened and that they were miracles in the strictest sense of the term, but even then I would not regard them as of more than peripheral importance in relation to the rest of the story. But it is altogether essential to believe that a certain man lived and taught as Jesus is described in the New Testament and died a cruel death at the hands of Roman soldiers and through the fury of those who most resented his teaching and influence.

This is bare and not very precise, but I have set out more carefully and fully in my paper 'The Person of Jesus' just what is the astonishing character of the person whose portrait takes shape for us in the gospel records. That might well have formed the fourth lecture in this series, but it has already been offered to the public as Chapter 8 of my *Persons and Life after Death*. I must refer you to what I have said in that paper for my own view of what stands out more distinctly in our impression of Jesus as he comes to us from the records against the background of all that happened before. There is little, if any, independent evidence of any essential matters, but I have maintained that this does not shake any of our confidence in the picture we have of an actual historical person without whom, as the distinctive person that shines out of the records, there would be no plausible explanation of the records themselves and the beginnings of Christianity. This is what I also made the main theme of the paper I read as my Address to the Society for the Study of Theology at Oxford and which has just been reproduced in part as an appendix to the previous lecture. How remarkable I take the person to be who emerges as the central figure in the New Testament, and how radically beyond any effective comparison with other notable figures and founders of great religions, will be more apparent in these writings and in the more ambitious work I have in progress to complete the trilogy of my Gifford Lectures which started with *The Elusive Mind*.

For the present I must content myself with the affirmation, or confession if you like, that the response of Jesus to all manner of persons and circumstances, to the wise and the foolish, to simple persons and sophisticated persons, to the maimed and the blind and the outcast, his sobriety and strength without any affectation, his tenderness and ease, and all that shapes itself, in the terms Professor Stewart Sutherland so finely indicates in the lecture mentioned earlier, so much in the way of perfection, in a rounded sacrificial life—all this puts him altogether in a class by himself, however meagre the evidence may seem in some ways, and well beyond anything we may expect to come about in the normal course of history.

This does not preclude attempts, of which there are many, to plot out the main stages in the public ministry of Jesus, as it is called. That is a matter for experts, but few would claim that it is possible to shape anything like a proper biography of Jesus in this way. What we have is enough to see his unfaltering step, and stand in ever-deepening amazement as our insightful imaginations bring out the astonishing sanity and wonder of his person.

But, in the second place, the Christian has also claimed, and is in my view entitled to do so, that the person we come to know in this way is not only unique, in the moral and religious respects most obviously involved, but comes to be recognised, in profound and committed contemplation, as the fulfilment of all that God had pre-eminently been doing in disclosing himself to men in their own experience and shaping their history by this intervention, not always in dramatic interludes but in the deepening sense of his presence educating their minds and hearts, extending and refining their sensitivity into the firm awareness of his boundless concern, for what sort of persons we are most of all, and the worth he puts on our relationship with him. This fulfilment is not, moreover, simply the completion of a work of divine disclosure and fellowship; it draws so much into itself that is so distinctive in the work of caring disclosure itself that we can only recognise it as God himself, in fully limited human form, at work in our midst making possible such a return and realisation of his care as to bring us eventually into that relation with himself, and with all in him, as will not be broken but continues, in modes other than our present existence, to expand into sanctified and ever enriching life, abundant beyond anything we can conceive in our limited and inadequate existence as we are now.

This seems to me to be the core of the Christian gospel, provided we stress enough the extremity of the divine sacrifice involved. It is easily travestied, as the history of Christianity and theological controversy proves. The question of the virgin birth itself had, I suspect, a good deal more to do with the issue of how this perfection could come about in the normal course of things, how distinctive incarnation is possible, than with the issues that became more prominent later of the possible transmission of sin and an essentially corrupted nature. These are also important issues in themselves, but I resist the temptation to repeat here what I have said about them elsewhere beyond strongly urging you, if you have not done so already, to read the splendid account of the origin of these ideas, in their more recognisable Christian form, by H. A. Wolfson in Chapter 6 of his *Religious Philosophy*.[1] There are of course intimations of such views in the Old Testament also, reflecting as much of it does the collectivist attitudes of early times. But these are also ideas which are progressively refined and corrected in the course of the process of divine illumination itself.

The main travesty of the Christian understanding of the 'passion' of Jesus has been due, in no small measure, to a too literal interpretation of certain metaphors about judgment and the fate of evil-doers, and most of all the notion of retributive punishment vicariously borne on behalf of all, for our unavoidable sinful state it is often thought, by Jesus. It does seem that many Christians have thought this the proper interpretation of the central themes and practices of their faith, including the notion of endless torment for those destined to be tormented for ever. Another factor has been the need to find some explanation and justification for the obvious disparity between the exhortations of Jesus and the normal way of life of Christians when the Christian community became established and organised within the Roman Empire. This is how we had the idea of a relative standard and an absolute standard not to be seriously expected of us, a doctrine which was given much prominence, with some appalling consequences in the Neo-Orthodox movement earlier this century.

I have maintained by contrast that the clue to God's

redeeming activity is better sought in our personal relations and in the cost of the genuine forgiveness by which a broken relation is mended. This will not take us the whole way. Nor are there any other metaphors which are completely adequate to so remarkable a giving as for God to suffer in a fully human form the pains and humiliations inflicted on Jesus. Attempts to explain in too explicit a manner how God could remain God, transcendent and unlimited, and yet fully undergo the experience of a limited being, being 'made man', are also usually wide of the mark and unhelpful. I do not mean that there is nothing we can helpfully say, but we need to be very cautious and to recognise where the limit of our understanding falls when dealing with matters which the evidence compels us to recognise, in all their mystery, without effectively seeing how they are possible. We are after all dealing with the relations of a truly transcendent God to ourselves and there is much, as I have so often stressed elsewhere, which we must recognise here though it goes beyond all comprehension.

It is much to be regretted that the travesties, often in their cruder forms, have been the basis of the impressions of the nature of Christianity, even among intelligent leaders of other religions. This has been a serious hindrance to mutual understanding, notwithstanding that the idea of divine retribution is far from absent in some form in other faiths. At the same time the distinctiveness of the once-for-all event and the genuineness of God incarnate, in the fullest possible sense, must not be overlooked or softened to achieve an easy accommodation. At the core of the Christian faith is an amazing claim which, if taken in its fullness, sets this religion apart from all others and claims for it an excellence and finality not to be found elsewhere.

It is for this reason that the Christian religion has always been a missionary one, out to convert others and bring them to the same way of thinking and the same experience. This has not been, originally and essentially, the case for all other influential religions. Buddhism, and the Quaker form of the Christian religion, have not always been markedly missionary in their outlook and practice, and Hinduism has usually been a very tolerant religion. Today most religions have acquired a new missionary fervour, but this is no doubt due in great measure to their renewed political allegiances. The Christian religion is pre-eminently, in its origins and in essentials, a missionary religion; and it cannot be true to itself when it abrogates or weakens its initial missionary concern to bring all others to the one true faith. It was so indeed in its background as well as in its origin, and it may be well to pause at this stage to bring the latter point out more fully.

The Christian religion had its cradle in the religion of the Hebrews, most of all as we find it in the Old Testament. The outstanding feature of the Hebrew faith was the insistence on one God—'Thou shalt have no other gods beside me'. There was no graver sin than idolatry, nor any more fiercely denounced. This one God tended quite often to be a tribal god, and to be opposed to the false and often feebler gods of other nations. He was the one Lord of Hosts, the God of Abraham, and Isaac and Jacob, the Lord God of Israel. But one God is willy-nilly the god of all; and as the Hebrews acquired their truly remarkable understanding of the genuine transcendence of God, his otherness and essential mystery, as seen in the classic story of the burning bush but quite as starkly in other places in the Old Testament, they came also to appreciate concurrently with this and almost as the obverse of the special understanding they had of it, that this remote, incomprehensible God was also near, 'in thy mouth and in thy heart', and that he was, not by accident or as a further property, but essentially, love, merciful and gracious, because he was the Lord; that, in later terms, creation and grace are the same thing, however strange this may seem to us; that they did not happen to coexist in God but were essentially the same thing.

In due course this understanding, with these curious paradoxes so unavoidable in being truly religious, ripened into the awareness that the one God, as unavoidably near as he was remote and strange, intervened or dealt with the life of the nation as a whole, not mainly in the external events of its history, but in its heart and experience, giving it a peculiar stance and resilience in its many tribulations and trials; and it came to be sensed also that this was for some ultimate purpose which no one could clearly discern but which, especially as it shaped itself more recognisably in the discernment of the prophet and the psalmist, extended well beyond the boundaries of the nation itself—in the language of a later time again, became a chosen vessel with its responsibility co-extensive with its privileges, that were not to be contained entirely within its own life. Everyone was within the Covenant because the one living God, 'the creator of the ends of the earth', was, in essentials and not fortuitously, merciful and gracious. The islands also rejoice.

With the coming of Jesus it became exceptionally and finally evident that there was no limit of land or race to what he had come to the world to establish, 'to seek and find that which was lost'. He would draw all to himself. He began his ministry in Galilee, around the lake, in Capernaum and in the synagogues, and he later taught in the Temple in Jerusalem; but, between these twin-poles of his ministry, we find him passing through Samaria, talking to people with whom the Jews had no dealings, and offering to a woman there the living water and teaching her that 'the hour cometh, when ye shall neither in this mountain, nor yet at Jerusalem, worship the Father' but 'in spirit and in truth'. The central character in one of the most notable and distinctive of his parables was a Samaritan. The word has now become a synonym for mercy even to the unbeliever. It was the faith of a Roman centurion that comforted him at a difficult time in his career, and it was to a Roman centurion that there was given the privilege to be the first to recognise and pronounce at the foot of his cross, 'Truly this man was the Son of God'.

When the small group of his followers came together in due course and began to take heart again in prayerful

expectation and found, to their amazement, that he was
alive and present to them again, and when they were
filled by the Holy Ghost on the day of Pentecost, we must
all have noticed how much the story emphasises the
variety of peoples present on that occasion—'Parthians
and Medes and Elamites, and the dwellers in Meso-
potamia, and in Judea, and Cappadocia (so prominent in
later doctrinal controversy), in Pontius and Asia, Phrygia
and Pamphylia, in Egypt and in the district of Lybia about
Cyrene, and strangers of Rome, Jews and proselytes,
Cretes and Arabians', almost all the known world at the
time. Recent scholarship has, moreover, made more
evident than ever how strong was the Hellenistic element
in Palestine at the time. Before long the first martyr died
under a shower of stones and with a vision of 'the glory of
God and Jesus standing on the right hand of God', and at
his side a young man among his persecutors into whose
heart, unknown to him then, fell the first seed of the
conviction that was to make him, Paul, the first and
greatest missionary to the gentiles. Through his witness
and that of many like him, the experience of the first
Christians entered the blood-stream of the Roman Empire
and spread to all parts of the known world. *We are
ourselves the children of this foreign mission*. They came to
our shores in Britain from the Continent and from Ireland,
met sometimes with resentment, sometimes made welcome; and in due course, when we learnt of it, the same
gospel was preached throughout your own continent. We
are the heirs of this missionary work.

There are times when we are apt to forget this. There is
a strong inclination to suppose, though we know well it is
not true, that it all started among ourselves, that Christianity was an essentially Western innovation, embodying
mainly Western values and perspectives. I suspect that
among many of my devout and insightful ancestors in my
beloved Wales there have been some who thought that
everything went on in the Bible in Welsh, although it is
little more than four hundred years since we had the First
Welsh translation and the magnificent hymns that came
out of that. These are our finest treasures, but they were

brought as the gift of others. We in the West are as much the debtors of the missionaries as any others. We did not invent the Christian faith; we received it; and it is for us to be equally determined in handing it on to others.

Against this general background let us now try to wind our way deeper to the heart of the essentially missionary aspect of our faith and our commitment to it. Why are the Christian Gospel and the Christian faith so essentially missionary ones? The answer is simple: because we have a distinctive truth to commend, and one that is of vital importance for the ultimate destiny of all. This moreover centres on the role and person of Jesus in the way indicated already. It is, as I have stressed, in our personal relation with him that we come to the ultimate fulfilment of ourselves in a sanctified relation with God. It is in this way that our restoration is complete and made secure beyond any further threat in fellowship with a living God which is the inexhaustible source of the continuing enrichment of life for which we are all destined. Sooner or later, in this existence or another, we have all to come within the same 'covenant' and fellowship through what God has done once and for all in Jesus Christ and pass through the judgment of his presence and costly reconciliation to the finality of our inheritance—and the sooner the better, whatever resources there may remain in God's providence for those who have never had, or have never benefited by, their opportunity in this life.

It is in this special relation with God in Jesus Christ that we find the ultimate purpose of our existence, and we shall never be fully right with ourselves or others until we achieve this, 'that in all things he might have the pre-eminence. For it pleased the Father that in him should all fullness dwell', so that 'at the name of Jesus every knee should bow' 'and that there is none other name under heaven given among men whereby we must be saved'.

All this is very familiar and very easy to proclaim before an audience like the present one, consisting largely I assume of committed Christians, or of persons sympathetic to us. But they are very far from being easy pronounce-

ments to make in other ways. They are difficult in at least
two main ways. Firstly, they are peculiarly difficult in
themselves. They are the most momentous assertions that
anyone could make. We tend to take them for granted,
but many philosophers of today—and some theologians
too—have found even the initial idea of 'one ultimate
transcendent source of all else there is' a totally meaningless one, not just implausible. This has much puzzled me,
as I have said on more than one occasion; for it is certainly
peculiarly hard to accept it that all there is just happens to
be, and leave it at that. But if the idea of infinite being,
beyond all beginning and end, is peculiarly hard to grasp,
how much more so the notion that this infinite existence
could also so limit itself as not merely to appear among
men, but to *be* a man. Stress has been laid more than once
in these lectures on the fully human character of Jesus,
having our needs, supported as we are, needing food and
drink and rest, experiencing joy and grief and friendship
and death with all that death means for us. But I will not
say more on that theme here, or on the heresies that come
about by seeking to avoid it. The evidence points to what
must have happened, in this one instance, whether we can
further account for it or not, and we can only proclaim it
with amazement and the wonder to which I hope
philosophers also are beginning to return. But this, to
which I shall return in further writings, is not what
concerns me especially now.

The doctrines I have mentioned are hard to proclaim
today for a further reason. They are out of accord with the
main tendencies and the drift of thought in our age. Our
culture seems to move in another direction. We are living
in an ecumenical age and the emphasis is placed on
accommodation and co-operation, on maintaining a broad
international outlook, on being tolerant and listening to
one another and on having a proper respect for one
another's differing views and practices, on removing the
barriers of colour, race, class and culture. We travel great
distances to meetings and conferences where we meet
people as gifted and experienced as ourselves; and who
are we, in that case, to lay down the law, to affirm that we

are right and everybody else is wrong. It is easy to have confident affirmations of faith among ourselves, but is there no danger that this may appear, and more than appear, narrow, self-assured, dogmatic, claiming that we and no others have the final answer to the ultimate problems and purpose of our existence? Are not the days for that sort of boldness well past?

This is a much more tempting line for us to take today because so many people of religions other than our own have actually settled in our midst, many of them splendid people. It is estimated that there are around a million Muslims in Britain today, and a great many Hindus and Sikhs and Buddhists; and the more aberrant forms of Christianity, as they seem to many, the Latter Day Saints and the Scientologists and their like, are extremely active. Some of these people adhere with apparently great devotion and sincerity to their faith and its practices in the face of many difficulties, and elicit much admiration for their perseverance and integrity, but are also very alert to every opportunity to propagate their faith and secure a better reception for their practices. They sometimes perform their acts of worship in the chapels and churches of which we have no longer any need. They set up new buildings and institutions for their own faith. There are many mosques in Britain today and no doubt in America, and many centres for meditation and the practices of Yoga. In California there is a recent Buddhist university, and Buddhism, while not originally or even essentially a missionary-minded religion, is much more alert to its opportunities today and on the move. This is happening in our midst and all around us. Other faiths are here and not in distant lands. Should we make it our business to quench their smoking flax and to resist or discourage the genuine spirituality which, in some measure at least, they display in days when materialism and discord are rampant? Should we not rather work our way closer to them, just as we are getting very much closer to one another in our various divisions within the Christian fold, Catholic and Protestant, Churchman and Non-conformist? Why should we harden ourselves in our differences? Is not the real enemy today, not another religion but outright irreligious worldliness?

This is undoubtedly the reaction of many thoughtful people today. Indeed, it is not long since I was speaking to one of the authors of *The Myth of God Incarnate* (see Appendix B) who said to me: 'You can't say these things any more (the kind of things I have been maintaining to be essential to the Christian faith), the others are all around us, in our midst'.

One thing surprised me, in this reaction of an experienced scholar, namely that he had almost forgotten that the other great religions, although not so evident in our own midst until lately, have flourished and been greatly influential for very many centuries in other countries, and some are very old indeed, as old as fairly reliable history goes. 'Other faiths' are not a recent phenomenon. Their challenge has been present to us from the start. It has only been intensified for us today, that is all.

At the same time, with the much more adequate knowledge and understanding we have today of other religions and the prominence accorded today to the study and discussion of them, in our colleges and on the media, it is more important than ever for us to consider very carefully and deeply what is to be our attitude towards them; and in these enlightened days with the spirit of good accord abroad, the proper course seems to be to subdue the note of firmness and the emphasis on distinctive and difficult affirmations which divide us and set us insisting that we are right and no others. Is it not variety of ways and practice that is suited to an enlightened age like our own? 'Live and let live' seems to be the appropriate maxim for times of so much stress and bitterness as ours.

We have, in fact, a very similar situation in regard to varieties of language and culture. One of the greatest threats to contemporary culture is that the circumstances of our times and especially the media of mass communication tend to impose a rigid and barren uniformity on all our creative activities. The way forward seems to be to maintain a healthy independence. That is very much the situation in my own little country of Wales. Our language and our culture are in dire peril, and we strain ourselves in every way possible, politically and socially, to maintain and extend them. Why? Is it because Welsh culture is superior to every other, and that there would be little left of culture and literature in the world with the demise of the Welsh language, and that it is only in Wales that anything of real worth is found? Of course not, that would be the most arrant nonsense. The strength and intensity of our plea and commitment lies in the fact that there are very distinctive features of Welsh culture, bound up closely with the language, and that its standard, in its artistry and in its penetration, is as high as we may find anywhere, and that for all this to pass for ever from the face of the earth, with the demise of the language, would be a loss beyond measure and break our hearts.

But it is the vigour and quality of our *own* culture that is at risk here. Other countries, great and small, have their distinctive excellence. There is the literature of Chaucer, Shakespeare, Milton, Wordsworth and the rich line of English prose writers, and the Scots and the Irish; there is French culture, and Italian culture in all its varieties, and great German literature, and Indian and Japanese culture. What a rich and novel experience it was for me to stay several months at Kyoto and see all the temples and screens and gardens, all with much which I had never encountered elsewhere. Who would grudge to all these their place and their special features and distinctiveness? We need of course to preserve the Welsh language and still greater efforts should be made to that end because of the plight of the language today, but we are not everybody and it would be totally absurd to try to make us all Welsh people and eliminate all other distinctive languages and cultures. The strength of our campaign in Wales today, and the basis of it, lies in the uniqueness of the language and the distinctiveness and variety of the culture which it makes possible.

And is it not in just this way that we must now begin to think of religion also? All power to those who wish to remain Christian; indeed let them declare that this is the best religion in the world. But it is quite another thing to say that everyone everywhere ought to be a Christian. Let the Hindu also be as loyal to his own religion, and the Muslim. There is room for us all, provided we are not so bold and opinionated as to say that our religion is the best religion for everyone. Let the Hindu and the Muslim, and others, keep to their own faith, and we in turn shall keep our own faith in Christ. There is merit in them all, and the best course is for us all to follow the faith which is natural to us in our own historical and cultural background, and so set aside disruptive wrangling and the smug self-assurance which sets our own faith and convictions ahead of all others. Is not the variety in our cultural existence the model for us also in religion, and are not toleration and restraint the real needs of our time rather than the authoritarian impudence which breeds friction and cruelty and the unreason of extravagant movements which have no tolerance for each other?

I was recently a member of a small group which contained some very eminent clerics. The conversation turned on the exceptional difficulties of missionary work today, though not with the depth of concern and anxiety that I would have expected. It is evident that there are quite exceptional difficulties at present. The missionaries find it very hard to get the necessary permission to stay in the countries where they work and where they have been outstandingly successful in the past. Even where there is freedom to worship according to your own choice, there are only limited facilities to propagate the Gospel and persuade men to leave their own religion and turn to that of Christ, and the native peoples have themselves to be very cautious. In the past it was possible for bold and determined missionaries to venture into wild and danger-ous places and face appalling difficulties and barbarous practices. Some were killed and others fell victims to various diseases for which there was no cure known at the time; others found the seed falling on good ground: they were allowed to remain and in time won the confidence and affection of those among whom they worked and saw the success of their own work. But today what opportunity have they, what prospects, however bold and determined, under the more rigorous systems of our times and contemporary methods of hindrance and detection? How far can you go without a visa or its equivalent, how long can you remain in hiding? Is not the greatest likelihood that you will be back on the next plane and lucky not to languish in prison?

There was recently a very strong move in India to suppress all forms of conversion and put it in the class of unfair influence or indoctrination and brain-washing. Talk of any sort of advance was thought to be unfair. This has been effectively resisted for the present, but it is a straw which shows which way the wind is blowing.

This was the subject of our conversation, and we wondered much what might be done in this trying situation. And then one of our members, a very outstanding and influential man in his own denomination, but I shall not name him—you would be surprised if I did— said: 'Why should we worry, they have their own religion'. Rarely have I been struck, in the course of such a conversation, with a deeper sense of sadness, indeed of very deep dismay.

And yet this is extensively the outlook of the world of today. It is also of course the outlook of many of the great religions themselves, notably Hinduism. Certain aspects of Hinduism come very close to what we believe as Christians, the theistic element in Hinduism being much stronger than used to be supposed. But the fundamental attitude of Hinduism is that there are many *ways*, some perhaps more effective than others, and that all lead eventually to the same place, to some consummation which is beyond them all. It does not matter eventually which way we choose, our destination is the same in the end—and that is altogether beyond our comprehension at present. There is no point in speaking of *The Way, The Truth* and *The Life*. And for this reason, Hinduism is on the whole, and where it has not been identified, as has happened so extensively today, with political forces, a very tolerant and liberal religion. It can indeed include us all and recognise the merits of the Christian way, although this is not the way for every man. The only difficulty which it meets in all this is that there are some who stubbornly maintain that there is in the end only one way.

And now to complete the picture of this challenge to the uniqueness and distinctiveness of the Christian faith, it is well for us to recall how much the general trend of thought in our own time tends in the same direction. Sometimes we have outright relativism, at other times more flexible and subtle variations on the same fundamental attitude. What seems to be especially rejected is the belief in objective truth and that we have often sound enough reasons for being confident that we have attained it. According to the prevailing fashion in the intellectual world, every truth is a truth *for me*, or for my class and contemporaries, or for my times, and a truth *for you* and for various societies and periods. Nothing is true in itself. The truth is in fact something which we ourselves make or choose; we decide what are to be its standards and what is to be believed. In the last resort it is a matter of a way of life, each one the equal of the other, provided we keep to the one way with consistency. Whatever religious practice is followed, then it is followed, and its justification is simply in the fact that it is practised. 'The game is played', according to the curious familiar idiom, and each game is as good as another, although everyone's game is not the game for us. The adherents to this view kick a lot against the pricks of the cruder forms of the relativism to which they seem impelled, and accordingly we find much ambiguity in their work. But it comes to the same thing in the end — to everyone his game, the sacrifice of animals or the sacrifice of Calvary; there is nothing to choose between them in the end, the way of Christ or the way of Hitler, to everyone his choice.

I have inveighed enough against this attitude in the second lecture in this book and have insisted how important it is, not only in religion, but in all walks of life, ranging from trivial day-to-day matters to concerns of the greatest moment for us, that the finality of the distinction between true and false be maintained. Nothing would be gained by seeking to develop that theme further here. I will only repeat that I consider the maintenance of it one of the greatest and most abiding tasks of philosophy. I also hold, along the lines already indicated, that we have ample reasons for believing that God was himself incarnate in Jesus, without being able to explain fully how this is possible. This has never been thought to be an easy affirmation, and much spiritual discernment is needed to appreciate it, a commodity not very plentiful in such a secular age as our own. I am fully convinced however that Christianity stands or falls with this claim, and that little remains that is properly distinctive of it once this central affirmation is surrendered.

But having stressed as vigorously as I can the finality of the distinction of true and false, and the reasonableness of claiming to have attained it in the matters of most ultimate concern to our destiny, including what seems uniquely true about Jesus and his relationship to God, it is equally important to indicate what is the proper way of affirming and propagating these ideas today. That has the same importance today as to understand them.

The first step is to acknowledge, as fully and handsomely as we can, the high attainments of other religions, and to do this without any suggestion of patronage or supercilious ascendancy. Whatever we may think of the superiority of the Christian faith, there is certainly a great deal we can learn from others and much in which they excel. Judaism was the cradle of our own religion and much would remain baffling to us without the Old Testament. There is likewise in other faiths a profound moral penetration and spiritual insight and sensitivity evident from earliest times to our own day, from the earliest Vedic hymns to the religious songs of Tagore. They also have their faults. Their adherents do not always dwell on the heights. They also become prey to empty formalities and automatic loyalties and tribal and family customs. They have been the breeding ground of much superstition and cruelty and hypocrisy. But are they much worse in this respect than ourselves? It is very difficult to say. How much genuine worship, how much genuine spiritual sensitivity does the ordinary Hindu display when he turns into his temple or makes his act of devotion and sacrifice, his *puja*, in his home? In my experience it has been very difficult to judge, any more than we can judge to what spiritual level we always attain in our churches and chapels. The impression which I retain, from reading and observation alike, is that there is a great deal of sincerity and genuine religious feeling mixed with a great deal of superstition and prejudice in the practices we observe in other religions. It would be very difficult to go much further than this, and it is certain that they themselves, as we do indeed ourselves, would say much the same thing about us.

The point of importance for us is that other religions, at their best and in the essentials of what they present, display an insight and an understanding of a very high order, and that we have also a great deal to learn from them, in genuine spirituality and in devotion, and very evidently today in the disciplines of meditation and the wholeheartedness it involves. The time is well past when we could simply talk of pagan darkness and crude worship of idols in speaking of other religions. I shall not easily forget the last time I attended a puja on a family day of festival in India and noted how naturally the tiniest tots prostrated themselves while the priest performed his office. It could not have meant much for them but it was hard not to suppose as they shut their eyes tight that they sensed something of the solemnity and holiness of the occasion. It is sometimes said today that China has become a religionless community. This is very hard to assess. One suspects that communism has not eliminated as much as is supposed. But before the communist revolution China was certainly one of the most religious parts of the world, and the basic factor in the more indigenous forms of Chinese religions is the idea of some power from beyond working within the world and finite life for goodness and justice; this has been a notable feature of their culture throughout the ages. In the spread of Buddhism into China and the intermixture of it with other practices the sense of spiritual reality was deepened in a way to which little justice is done either in China or in Japan or Sri Lanka or other places where Buddhism is now powerful and often still understood in the West in completely sceptical and negative ways. Without seeking here to go into details, we find in Buddhism and Hinduism, and very evidently in the more semitic religion of the Muslims, an intensity and depth of spiritual experience and worship of an impressively high order. Nothing could be more mistaken than to cast these religions aside as useless and wholly misleading aberrations. We know much better than that today, although it does not follow that we place the same estimation on them all or try to cover up their faults and failures, any more than our own.

It is indeed deeply regrettable, as we can well see today, that our attitude to other religions in the past has been extremely biased and unintelligent, as if nothing but utter moral and spiritual darkness could be found outside of Christianity. God has spoken in diverse times and places, and not solely to the Hebrews. The late Austin Farrer observed, in a remark which I have often found myself quoting: 'Men knew that God was God before they knew that he would send his only begotten son into the world'. Unhappily it was not in that spirit that we used to study other religions. When they were studied at all it was as part of the preparation of missionaries and preachers and to help them to see how utterly false and useless were all the practices of benighted heathens. This stupid and ill-informed attitude persisted long into this century in the works of men of the highest influence and prominence like Karl Barth and his disciple Hendrik Kraemer. Indeed it was a powerful ingredient in the faith of many a Christian in times past that those who had not got to know and accept Christ went at once at their death to ever-lasting punishment, including those who had never had a proper opportunity to learn about him. There can be no doubt that many Christians have believed this, and it is strange for us today to recall that the only amelioration of this horrendous doctrine which even so fine a thinker as St Augustine would allow would be that God, in his mercy, would not allow the flames to be quite so fierce for little children.

A short while ago I read of someone who had made a calculation of how many souls had gone to perdition in this way since the end of the 1939–45 war, making his estimate on the way he calculated, in terms of those who did not profess the Christian faith today, including the very great majority who never had the slightest opportunity to hear it. Such a procedure, and its presuppositions, are as purblind and absurd as they are far-removed from the spirit and person of Jesus Christ.

Without more elaboration here, it is evident that it is of the utmost importance for us to acknowledge and to understand the merits and high achievements of those who are not of the same faith as ourselves, both in the study of their scriptures and of their practices. We ought to be glad of all that they have to offer us and to teach us and to learn from them, and we need to be fair and careful in our criticisms of them. This does *not* mean that we abstain from criticism. It will be a great advantage to some Eastern religions to have to face more boldly than they have done hitherto the challenge of the empiricist and linguistic philosophy with which religious people have had to deal in the West, and they might learn to discard many foolish features in the process. But this ought not to dim in any way our appreciation of the high achievements and of all we may appreciate better in our encounter with them at all levels.

It will be a great advantage to set out how much is common to the various religions; and there are better ways of doing this than a crude syncretism. Our aim should be not so much to find out what is literally common to various religions as to discover what I have elsewhere called 'points of convergence', those places where our consciousness and sensitivity inclines towards the same basic and creative insights. We shall all find this a very great blessing and a refinement of spirit and attitude, especially if we look deeper than formal pronouncements.

I had myself a very fine experience of this fairly recently.

I spent some months in Japan leading a seminar or discussion group on basic religious questions with a number of Christian and Buddhist scholars who met regularly for this purpose. I agreed with some reluctance but they were extremely patient with my very limited experience of their own religion. I do not know if I ever had a richer cultural experience. The Japanese excel at careful discussion and the technique of proper controversy. They are never verbose but patient and acute in the extreme. We sat around a table, sometimes in complete silence, and then someone would make an observation, to be capped by another, breaking through together, almost with the concentration and in the spirit of a game of chess, to the heart of the truth or making it clearer where we misunderstood one another, or only half understood. And in this way, being taken by one kind friend after another to visit their temples and to meet and question, in a very free and uninhibited way, some of the Masters in the religious orders, and also by spending some hours sharing in the meetings for meditation, I arrived at a much better understanding than I had previously had of the secret and strength of this strange religion. The emptiness of which they spoke so much was also fullness, but on neither side did we ever try to hide the differences, some very deep ones, which divided us.

Our meetings were in a way acts of worship themselves —what in Wales is called a 'Seiat', and I am very certain that meetings of this sort, with the atmosphere subdued but rarefied for us to be sensitive to spiritual things, will have a very important place in the religion of the future. It is in this way, by 'spiritual discernment', and without any diminution of the sharpness and genuineness of our understanding that we came to appreciate those points of convergence I have spoken of already.

At the same time, to show respect for one another and meet in a fair commitment to understand and appreciate one another's achievement is no justification for holding back on the matters of final importance which we believe we have laid hold upon in our own faith. Genuine toleration does not in any way mean that we have to be silent where there is a difference of opinion and conviction. That would be a very feeble form of toleration. As I have already observed, it is not always easy to express a contrary opinion, to be bold enough to say, sensibly and courteously but firmly as occasion arises, to our Muslim friend who kneels with so much deep devotion in the congregation at the Mosque that it is in the name of Jesus that every knee should bow in the end, and that it is in the fellowship of his suffering that we come to our complete and final relation with God and the full richness of the reconciliation and sanctification which will maintain us in the vigour and splendour of the inexhaustible resources, in point of character and spirituality, and all the colourful fullness of the life prepared for us hidden with God in Christ.

It is indeed as regrettable as anything can be that there has been so much distortion of these matters, just as it is also so very lamentable that so many of our brethren are so willing to dispense with them in the interest of an easy and costless toleration on the surface. If 'the preaching of the cross' is an offence, this is also a rare part of the fellowship of his sufferings. Let us seek all wisdom and sincere gentleness: let us try to go as deeply as we can in mutual understanding into one another's excellences; but let us not be reluctant to hold on to the things that others will not admit or be slack in offering to others the unspeakable riches which we believe we have found in Jesus Christ. If the price is high, let us not forget the price which he had to pay himself.

It is my belief that we shall find no perfect ordering of either our society or our personal existence until we come into right relation with the God who is to be found in Jesus Christ. This is not an extra, an option, but an essential condition of our flourishing. There is more need to be aware of it today than at any time, not because our times, in spite of all the horrors of which we read every day, are obviously worse than times past (what unambiguous standards are there to apply on such a scale?) but because the circumstances and complexities of our life today have forced us into such a crisis of conflict and survival that we have little chance of meeting it without the best and fullest resources of all that is best in our nature and achievements, and it is in Christ that we find these. 'For it pleased the Father that in him all goodness should dwell, and some new wonder of this person will continue to come to light as a source of life and enhancement. When we have weighed up all, what we come up with in the end is 'that there is no other name'; and just for this reason, to testify with more resolution and sacrifice than ever, to bear witness, at home and abroad, is more essential than at any time.

The one thing that would transform our society and its prospects today would be to have a company of committed young people, possessed as in times past with the same appreciation of holy things and, with mind and intelligence fully alert, to perceive in the new forms appropriate to today and in the fullness of the life we have now, the excellence of the Gospel of Christ, and to feel the same unrestrained urge to declare it, in word and deed, in the forms and media most appropriate to our age. Our task is not to go back, least of all blindly, to things of the past, nor indeed just to move forward, but to find that Christ again is 'the author and finisher of our faith'. We shall grow with him in our enlightened understanding of him.

The narrow outlook, the positiveness of obstinate and stubborn people of limited thought and understanding, may succeed and have good speed for a while. But that cannot last, and that sort of victory is little worth having. It is a time of many strange and often absurd new religions, some crazy in the extreme even though they bear the name of Christ, some of sheer and repulsive paganism. That is not how we have learned Christ, and it is not by twisting and perverting, least of all by borrowing 'the Name' for low and unworthy ends, that we shall serve our age. *It is the enlightened Gospel of Christ that we need, not the religion of the aboriginal.* This is what our faith culminates in, and those who have glimpsed the inexhaustible wonder of his person, and all the richness which this opens out, need feel no embarrassment or inhibition in proclaiming this Gospel anywhere.

At the same time it is well for us to recall what is the real character of the true missionary. We find the exemplar of it in the first and greatest of all missionaries, St Paul. You will remember his own description of the trials he had to endure and his constant concern about the small societies he had founded and the ease with which they were led astray:

> In journeys often, in perils of waters, in perils of robbers, in perils by my own countrymen, in perils by the heathen, in perils in the city, in perils in the wilderness, in perils of the sea, in perils among false brethren; in weariness and painfulness, in watchings often, in hunger and thirst, in fastings often, in cold and nakedness. Besides these things that are without, that which cometh upon me daily, the care of all the churches.[2]

It is this determination and endurance that will alone suffice today; and we have also a finer and completer pattern than St Paul himself, that which caused this remarkable missionary himself to declare (and St Paul was not by nature a modest person) 'For I determined not to know anything among you save Jesus Christ and him crucified'.

He remains the great healer of all, not because an impersonal justice sends us to perdition if we reject him, but because it is only in himself, 'who thought it not robbery to be equal with God' but also disclosed to us the unlimited grace which is the very essence of the Infinite, that we have that complete access by one spirit to the Father and that fellowship which makes us whole as individuals and societies.

This is not for us as a society apart, nor to anyone in strict isolation, but for all in the bonds of the same love and the same fellowship in the Kingdom. And the more we fall into the conflicts and the prodigality of the life that is not sustained in this way, the more urgent is the need to proclaim that salvation which is alone abiding and unshakable. Superficial joviality will not attain this, nor the easy adaptation of Christian themes to popular entertainment. There must be truly missionary work of a wholly committed and fully intelligent nature—perhaps heroic is the proper word, so grim is our situation. To frighten people with antiquated talk of hell-fire is totally counterproductive. It produces either fanaticism or derision. I have said little or nothing about the modes or techniques of such missionary work today. We should certainly not be averse to learning from other successful movements, even though much that they commend is offensive to us. It is not a subject on which I feel competent to say much myself. But of the need and the urgency there can be no doubt at all.

There is no ultimate fulfilment other than that in Christ. Let us then take heart to offer this afresh to a world and a period that stands so much in need of it. May he bless our work and give us his holy presence.

'He who testifieth these things saith, Surely I come quickly. Amen. Even so, come Lord Jesus'.

NOTES

1. H. A. Wolfson, *Religious Philosophy* (Harvard University: Bilknap Press, 1961).
2. St Paul, 2 Cor., 11, 26.

Appendix A: Interfaith Services

I have little experience of these services. Even so the reader of this book may find it helpful to reflect on the following four occasions in my own experience. I shall just describe them and leave the reader to reflect on them for himself.

(i) Many years ago, long before I had moved from my Chair in straight philosophy at Bangor to take up the responsibility for the history and philosophy of religion at the University of London, I had interested myself in 'other religions' and written slightly about them. This, I suspect, was the reason why I was invited to take part in what seemed to me then a very exciting conference at a beautiful centre in the New Forest in Hampshire. The most generous arrangements were made for us who were invited to lecture and a good company of people was assembled. Socially and scenically nothing could be more agreeable. The speakers were chosen to represent different religions. The Imam of the mosque at Woking was there, and the President of the Buddhist Society at the time, Professor Werblowsky, spoke for the Jews and Professor Ayer for agnostics, and others. The prospect was a very exciting one, and I had later the privilege of editing the main papers as a series for the *Hibbert Journal*. In point of friendliness nothing could have been better; we all got on together extremely well, but we never really *met*. Each speaker told us very much what we knew already from books, and we answered questions in very predictable ways. Controversy is not what I had expected, and I would not have welcomed much of it. But I had assumed that here was a splendid opportunity for *probing*, for seeking to find out better, in the idiom of today, what makes us tick. Nothing could have been more disappointing or frustrating, even in private conversation or walks together. We remained with the secure shelter of our own convictions and commitments. Nothing happened of the slightest importance to me during the whole of this week, and my own thoughts never moved forward at all. Perhaps the blame was partly my own. I may have naively expected too much and been too retiring myself, but I returned home with a sense of deep frustration.

(ii) There was held some years ago at the Anglican chapel of King's College, London an inter-faith service. This was some surprise to me as the institution in question was a very conservative one in ritual practice. But some members of our Council, including the present Dean of Westminster, were very interested in the idea of inter-faith services. There was great interest and a large congregation filled the chapel. The proceedings were started, if memory serves me right, by the Dean of the College conducting a portion of the normal Anglican service, followed by the Imam of the mosque at Woking giving a brief Friday sermon, then a Hindu and a Buddhist priest. The Buddhist began with a loud intoning of the sacred word *Om*. There had been no preparation for this service and only the smallest handful of students of religions had the faintest notion of the history and significance of the word. The result was a titter, barely subdued by angry glances; and this was the general tone of the meeting throughout. There was little sense of a common spiritual purpose or of instruction in one another's thoughts and practice. As a spiritual occasion it was a total failure.

If such services are thought proper they need a great deal of preparation beforehand. On the whole I don't think they are likely to be helpful.

(iii) On the third occasion I was a visitor at Visvabarhati University, Santiniketan. It was Christmas Day, and a service had been arranged in the evening for Hindus and

Christians—and indeed, from what I could see, for any
who cared to attend—in a lovely hall open on one side to
the gentle evening air. It began without preliminaries or
fuss with delightful songs and music from Tagore,
followed by impressive readings from the Bible, especially
St John's Gospel. There was nothing in these which a
Hindu could not wholeheartedly say. It was a simple
service but the sense of devotion was very moving and
meaningful. The meeting closed with a candle procession,
and all dispersed to their homes. This had undoubtedly
been a fine religious occasion, and the memory of it will
always remain a tender one. But it was *at a price*. The price
was that nothing discordant to either side had been
included. We could all share in the Tagore songs and
there was no part of the New Testament which a Hindu
could not say in his own way. There is a place for
meetings of this kind, but they can also be deceptive, for
they depend on leaving out matters, of Christian belief
especially, which can in no way be absorbed into
Hinduism.

(iv) The fourth occasion was the one already alluded to in
Japan, not conceived as a devotional occasion but where
there was none the less a deep sense of spiritual probing
and of bringing differences into the open, without
rancour or hostility (by no means an easy achievement, as
the history of Christianity shows only too well).

   I will close this appendix with a very moving passage at
the end of an article on 'Theology and Religious Studies'
by Professor A. D. Galloway. He writes:

   I was once invited to attend the Friday service at a
   mosque. As I stood reverently on the side-lines as it
   were, to my utter astonishment, an awesomely dignified
   and authoritative beturbaned Muslim beckoned me to
   come and share his prayer mat with him. With some
   misgivings and embarrassment I did so. I said my
   prayers in my way. He said his in his way. When it was
   all over and we went to collect our footwear, we looked
   at one another and knew we had shared something.

what had we shared? Because of the language barrier our conversation was restricted to an exchange of a few polite greetings and salutations. So we could not discuss the question. That is perhaps as well. Certainly he had not blunted the edges of his proud Islamic faith on my account. The proud jaunt of his turban and the fiercely quizzical glint in his eye showed that. Certainly I had not qualified the Christian content of my faith to accommodate him. That would not have been honourable. He would not have thanked me for it if I had. Yet we knew that we had shared something. What was it? I think it was the acknowledgement that the truth is one, though we are many and diverse. It was the acknowledgement that the truth is that to which we owe the debt of humility and reverence. It is upon this that the unity and integrity of our discipline ultimately depends'.[1]

These various occasions will in my view bear some reflection.

NOTE

1. A. D. Galloway, 'Theology and Religious Studies', *Religious Studies*, vol. II (1975) p. 165.

Appendix B: A note on Professor Hick's views

I have not referred explicitly to the views of Profesor John Hick as advanced in the closing chapter of *The Myth of God Incarnate*. This is mainly because the substance of my reaction to his views is found in Lecture 4. But a brief additional note may be in order.

In the first place I fail to agree with the phrase, used more than once 'the largely unknown man of Nazareth'. I find it difficult to understand how Hick can speak, as he does at times, with great tenderness and appreciation, about Jesus if Jesus is as unknown as he makes him out to be.

Secondly, Hick points out, rightly, that Jesus meets many different needs and that different pictures of him emerge. There seems to me to be nothing disconcerting about this, provided the pictures cohere or correct one another. We have various glimpses of a personality who is too remarkable to be regarded as a normal finite phenomenon and too full of God to be anything other than God. To treat him as simply another extraordinary teacher and prophet does not rest easily upon us, not because of centuries of being taught otherwise, but because meditative living with the evidence (the 'traditions' as Hick prefers to call them) brings with it irresistibly the conviction, the vision or insight if you like, of the one consciousness united here with the living God.

Hick is very much impressed with the comparison with Buddhism. Buddha was not regarded at first, not indeed for many centuries, as a divine figure, and when this came about more explicitly with the rise of Mahāyāna Buddhism it was as one figure among many, 'the most

recent', 'an incarnation of the heavenly Buddhas, pro-
jections of their life into the stream of this life'. In due
course the heavenly Buddhas become 'one with the
Absolute, as in Christianity the eternal son becomes one
with God the father.'

One comment which this invites is that it was centuries
later that this transformation of Buddha took place, and
that it still does not make the 'Absolute' fully incarnate
himself. Professor Hick is labouring under the impression, common to the other thinkers on whom I have
commented, that it was a slow process of theological
thinking, over some centuries, that gave rise to the idea of
the divinity of Christ, whereas it seems instead to have
been the immediate reaction of those close to him at the
time. Theologians tried to *explain* this, and often tried to
explain too much, but they were struggling with the
difficulties of giving an exhaustively rational account of
what transcends complete understanding on our part.

The fact that other figures than Jesus are accorded
divine status does not prove that the case is equally strong
in each instance. I am little tempted to accord it except in
the quite extraordinary case of Jesus, and this in spite of
attempts to think of him otherwise. Hick writes 'Thus in
Jesus's presence, we should have felt that we are in the
presence of God—not in the sense that the man Jesus
literally *is* God, but in the sense that he was so totally
conscious of God that we could catch something of that
consciousness by spiritual contagion.' My own experience
has been different. It is not a case of 'catching something
by contagion' but of feeling the holy presence of God
himself in all the glimpses we have of this remarkable
person in all the multifarious situations presented to us,
including above all the circumstances of his death as they
appear in the records of it.

Professor Hick labours also under the impression,
which I have been trying to correct in Lecture 4, that 'God
can only be adequately known', on the more traditional
views, through Jesus, and that the whole religious life of
mankind beyond the stream of Judaic-Christian faith is
thus by implication excluded as lying outside the sphere

of salvation.' There can be little doubt that this view has been held and has done great harm. But one does not have to deny the insights of other religions and their genuine contact with God, or all that we have to learn from them, as I have stressed, in order to ascribe to Jesus a distinctive role in the final relationship of man with God. Those who have not had the opportunity to appreciate this will be found, in God's grace and providence, the means to do so somehow, in his concern to draw all men to himself and thereby open up the riches of an existence barely conceivable to us now. Hick declares: 'But what we cannot say is that all who are saved are saved by Jesus of Nazareth'. If this means that there is no light outside the Christian faith, or that those who do not embrace it (or hear of it) are subjected to punishment and torment, then that is indeed a horrible doctrine; and its continuation can only do great harm. But insistence on the distinctiveness of Jesus does not carry with it this kind of exclusiveness or commit us to see Christianity within this 'pluralistic setting'. We do need to 'draw together in the face of increasing secularisation throughout the world'. But we can draw together with tolerance of one another's differences and a claim to insist on proclaiming those ingredients in our belief which are not acceptable to others. Surely this is what true toleration means, and I have not found it difficult to practise this. That the situation may be much complicated by political issues that merge with religious ones, is also true; and this brings its own complications and difficulties. This is part of the cross which all witnesses to the truth have to bear today.

That there are ingredients in Christian traditions which we need to revise or to dispense with altogether is also true, but this does not mean that we need or are able to dispense with 'the interpretative framework built around him (Jesus) by centuries of Western thought', or that our own Western 'mythology' must be allowed to 'function as an iron mask from within which alone Jesus is allowed to speak to mankind'.

It is, I think, very significant that at one stage (p. 178) Professor Hick speaks of 'mystery' rather than mythological idea. This seems to me to get much nearer the truth. The Christian tradition has always treated the incarnation as a mystery, something to which our own intelligences can never be wholly attuned. I have stressed more than once the dangers of seeking to bring this supreme act of God within the full ambit of our own minds, and many of the logos doctrines to which Hick also refers, fall foul of the truth in this way. But it is understandable that perplexed theologians should err in this fashion. The alternative is not a blind fideism either, but a matter of living imaginatively with the available evidence until the vision dawns, and conveying it to others in as sensitive, but firm, a way as we can, as an urgent need, in my view the *most* urgent need, of the world today. Pluralism will not suffice. The truth is what we have to seek and proclaim; and as I see it, there is nothing more important, here or hereafter, than to realize our special fellowship with God in Christ through what God did, after speaking to us in various times and places, by taking his own stance in our midst, and in the most utter destitution we endure, once and for all in Jesus—not 'the unknown man of Nazareth' but the one we astonishingly come to know as a living presence in living committed lives with the evidence available to us spiritually and sensitively grasped.

I have not dealt as fully as I would like with all the aspects of Professor Hick's pluralistic and 'global' theology. But I hope to return to this and related theories in a more exhaustive way in another work in preparation.

Index of Names

Index of Subjects

aesthetic experience, 2
agnostic, 1, 3, 10
agnostic philosophies, 9
ahimsa, 45
antinomies, 4
a priori knowledge, 6, 14, 16
Aramaic, 2
arguments, traditional, 3

Buddhism, 27, 82, 88, 95, 96, 107, 108,
Buddhists, 88, 98

Chalcedon, Council of, 56, 59
Copernican Revolution, 37
corporate being, 52

deist, 27
deistic way, 27
divinity of Jesus, 21, 27, 29, 30, 34, 49, 54, 59, 60

emanation, 60
empirical critics, 6, 7, 97
empirical evidence, 36
empiricism, 6

Fall, doctrine of the, 42
fideism, 32–3, 110
French culture, 90

German literature, 90
Gnostic ideas, 55
Greek, 66
guilt, 53, 75
    collective, 12
    sense of, 13

Hamlet, 70
Hebrew faith, 83
Hebrew history, 17
Hebrews, 83, 96
Hinduism, 83, 92, 96
Hindus, 88, 91, 95
Humanism, 21, 22
Humanists, 38
    secular, 23, 28

'Idea of the Holy', 27
Idealism, post-Hegelism, 29–31
Idealist philosophies, 66
Indian culture, 90
Irish, 90
Islam, 29
'I–thou relation', 3

Japanese culture, 90
Jew, 66
Judaism, 94

Latter Day Saints, 88
Liberal Theology, 31
'limit situations', 4

Marxist purpose in history, 45
metaphysical reflection, 2
metaphysics, 2
monism, 30, 31
moral experience, 2
Muslims, 29, 66, 88, 91, 96, 99
mystical experience, 1
mystical philosophers, 18
mystics, 26
myth, 35–7